SCARS

Social Fictions Series

Series Editor
Patricia Leavy
USA

The *Social Fictions* series emerges out of the arts-based research movement. The series includes full-length fiction books that are informed by social research but written in a literary/artistic form (novels, plays, and short story collections). Believing there is much to learn through fiction, the series only includes works written entirely in the literary medium adapted. Each book includes an academic introduction that explains the research and teaching that informs the book as well as how the book can be used in college courses. The books are underscored with social science or other scholarly perspectives and intended to be relevant to the lives of college students—to tap into important issues in the unique ways that artistic or literary forms can.

Please email queries to pleavy7@aol.com

International Editorial Advisory Board

Carl Bagley, University of Durham, UK
Anna Banks, University of Idaho, USA
Carolyn Ellis, University of South Florida, USA
Rita Irwin, University of British Columbia, Canada
J. Gary Knowles, University of Toronto, Canada
Laurel Richardson, The Ohio State University (Emeritus), USA

Scars

A Black Lesbian Experience in Rural White New England

By

A. Breeze Harper
University of California, Davis, USA & The Sistah Vegan Project

SENSE PUBLISHERS
ROTTERDAM / BOSTON / TAIPEI

A C.I.P. record for this book is available from the Library of Congress.

ISBN 978-94-6209-759-9 (paperback)
ISBN 978-94-6209-760-5 (hardback)
ISBN 978-94-6209-761-2 (e-book)

Published by: Sense Publishers,
P.O. Box 21858, 3001 AW Rotterdam, The Netherlands
https://www.sensepublishers.com/

Printed on acid-free paper

Cover figure by Sarah Juanita Dorsey

COPYRIGHT NOTICE

TABLE OF CONTENTS

TABLE OF CONTENTS

ACKNOWLEDGMENTS

Sarah Dorsey, thank you for dedicating so much love and time in order to create a beautiful painting for this book cover. When I first saw the final painting, my heart and mind were blown away by your brilliance. You translated my manuscript into an artistic masterpiece. I look forward to collaborating with you more in the future.

Sister Jayne Simon, your intense enthusiasm for *Scars* was amazing. Thank you so much for being a strong influence in my life.

Patricia Leavy, I appreciate how you enthusiastically took *Scars* under your wing. Thanks for seeing how well *Scars* aligns with *Sense's* social fiction goals. Thank you even more for being a vangaurd in the fields of social fiction and qualitative research studies.

Kia Hayes, the time you spent copy editing this book was amazing. You helped me take character and scene developments to the next level.

Maya Thau-Eleff, thank you so much for coming into my life at the last minute. You have done a phenomenal job as a proofreader.

Melissa Haile, thank you for being a strong and encouraging sister. If it had not been for you, I really don't think I could have finished this book. You were truly my muse for the final stages of this project!

Oliver Zahn, thank you for being a supportive and inspiring husband.

Angela Y. Davis, thank you for being my mentor from afar. Your scholarship has helped me think about the intersections of oppressions and liberation in profound ways.

Gwen Fortune, thank you for spending time to read through *Scars.* You have been my mentor for a very long time. It was you who helped me to understand the power of telling stories of the African Diaspora, through the medium of novel writing.

Zenju Earthlyn Manuel, *Scars'* themes of forgiveness and trying to love one's self (as well as 'the enemy') were greatly influenced by having read your book *Seeking Enchantment.* Thank you for being a wonderful spiritual advisor.

Holly Marie Eaton, your pursuit of creative writing, as a profession, has been very inspiring to me. Thank you for reading my first completed manuscript when we were undergrads at Dartmouth College in the 1990s.

Talmadge Harper, thank you for being an awesome twin brother and understanding me so well.

Thank you mom and dad for allowing me to become a voracious bookroom. I owe this to your dedication to my education and taking me to the library and my favorite used book stores as often as possible.

PREFACE

Scars is a novel about whiteness, racism, and breaking past the normative boundaries of heterosexuality, as experienced through eighteen year old Savannah Penelope Sales. Savannah is a Black girl, born and raised in a white, working class, and rural New England town. She is in denial of her lesbian sexuality, harbors internalized racism about her body, and is ashamed of being poor. She lives with her ailing mother whose Emphysema is a symptom of a mysterious past of suffering and sacrifice that Savannah is not privy to. When Savannah takes her first trip to a major metropolitan city for two days, she never imagines how it will affect her return back home to her mother ... or her capacity to not only love herself, but also those who she thought were her enemies. *Scars* is about the journey of friends and family who love Savannah and try to help her heal, all while they too battle their own wounds and scars of being part of multiple systems of oppression and power. Ultimately, *Scars* makes visible the psychological trauma and scarring that legacies of colonialism have caused to both the descendants of the colonized and the colonizer ... and the potential for healing and reconciliation for everyone willing to embark on the journey.

As a work of social fiction born out of years of critical race, Black feminist, and critical whiteness studies scholarship, *Scars* engages the reader to think about USA culture through the lenses of race, whiteness, working-class sensibilities, sexual orientation, and how rural geography influences identity. What makes this novel unique is its emphasis on Black and lesbian teen experience of whiteness and racism within rural geographies. Often, interrogations of whiteness and socio-economic class are left out of popular LGBTQ literature. My intention with *Scars* is to fill this gap by creating emotionally intense dialogues among four primary characters: Savannah Penelope Sales, Davis Allen, Esperanza Perez, and Erick Roberts.

Davis Allen is one of Savannah's best friends. A straight white male who grew up on a rural dairy farm in Savannah's home town, Davis and Savannah have been close friends since they were toddlers. Davis is the only white friend Savannah has ever chosen to develop a close friendship with. When Davis and Savannah interact with each other, the intimacies of their conversations reveal an interesting dynamic: Davis's perception of reality manifests from what Savannah has marked as "a privileged point of entry": white, male, lower-middle class, and straight. Davis can never experience Savannah's embodied experience as a Black lesbian. Growing up in a country that has institutionally legitimized whiteness and heterosexuality as 'normal', Davis's white and straight identity limits him to superficially interpreting Savannah's verbal hostility as nothing more than stereotypical "angry Black female" banter.

The second theme developed in *Scars* is the irreconcilable differences that Erick Roberts and Savannah endure in their rocky new friendship. Erick and Savannah both identify as same gender loving, however, that is where similarities between them end. Their frequent antagonistic verbal intercourses deconstruct the common myth that being gay or lesbian means they will instantly connect emotionally to each other as comrades in the same battle against homophobia. The exhaustive energy it takes for both to maintain their volatile relationship has its roots in Erick's oblivion to the fusion of his upper-middle class status and his white male privilege when attempting to advise Savannah about being and coming out as a [Black, poor, and rural] lesbian.

The third and more subtle theme developed in *Scars* centers on how Savannah's perception of oppression is positioned within a geopolitically global North perspective. Savannah never acknowledges her privilege as a USA national; only her *lack* of privileges as a non-white person. She considers herself revolutionary in thought in comparison to the people living in the provincial town she grew up in. Simultaneously, she has no awareness of her perpetuation of inequality outside of the USA; for example, Savannah is unaware of how many people of color outside of the USA are exploited so she can buy cheap coffee, chocolate, and Coca-Cola. Esperanza Perez, a key character, is one of her best friends. Esperanza, a vegan and fair trade anti-globalization activist who originally grew up in Guatemala, visits Savannah from college. Through honest and heartfelt dialogues with Esperanza, Savannah's oblivious understanding of her geopolitical Northern privilege is revealed. I hope to engage the reader to empathize with Savannah's realistic struggles with "whiteness as the invisible norm in the USA," while also addressing the need for Savannah to engage deeper into social injustice by encompassing and linking Black struggles and USA racism to a broader range of social and ecological inequalities throughout the world.

Born out of my Dartmouth College thesis social research in feminist geography, award winning Masters work at Harvard University, and my dissertation work at the University of California-Davis, *Scars* emphasizes how rural geographies of whiteness can impact the consciousness and young identity development of non-white youth who seemingly 'don't belong' in rural settings of whiteness and hetero-normativity; yet, the reader sees during Savannah's trip to her first major metropolitan city, she is very much out of place. Furthermore, Savannah contrasts the mainstream media stereotype that the "authentic Black experience" is from heterosexual Blacks raised in predominantly urban landscapes. Even though the critical theory in this novel has been translated into creative writing format, it is notable that *Scars* was significantly influenced by a strong canon of Black critical thinkers and writers stemming back to W.E.B. DuBois. My choice to title the book *Scars* reflects the legacy of Black anti-colonialist Frantz Fanon and his intense dedication to making visible, the psychological trauma and scarring that colonialism, white supremacy, and racism have caused to both the colonized and the colonizer. Furthermore, this book continues the traditions of bell hooks, Audre Lorde, and Octavia Butler who have written extensively about the 'the problem of the color line.' However unlike Fanon and DuBois' more heteronormative and masculinist analyses, hooks, Lorde, and Butler have complicated the 'problem of the color line' with intersectional analysis of gender and sexual orientation.

Scars can be used as a springboard for discussion, self-reflection and social reflection for students enrolled in American Studies, Sociology, Women's Studies, Sexuality Studies, African

American Studies, human geography, LGBTQ studies and critical whiteness studies courses, or it can be read entirely for pleasure.

A. Breeze Harper

PROLOGUE

Once riding in old Baltimore,
Heart-filled, head-filled with glee,
I saw a Baltimorean
Keep looking straight at me.

Now I was eight and very small,
And he was no whit bigger,
And so I smiled, but he poked out
His tongue, and called me, "Nigger."

I saw the whole of Baltimore
From May until December;
Of all the things that happened there
That's all that I remember.

—Countee Cullen
"Incident," 1925[i]

***

"Look at that skinny little nigger."

    First day of school and these words greeted me as I entered the halls of East Lebanon Middle and Senior High school. It had not been the era of Jim Crow nor the Civil Rights Movement in the small town of East Lebanon, Connecticut. There were no 'for colored only' signs or separate drinking fountains like during the era of my grandparent's childhood. However, the n-word had found its way into the year 2000, revealing that as we entered the new millennium, time had little to do with change. This memory reminds me of when hard times would befall our household, Mama used to say with dark sullen eyes, "This too, shall pass."

    Nearly seven years later, I would be lying if I said I didn't think about that day and that word on a weekly basis. I know, with the utmost confidence, that most brown and Black people will never forget the first time they were verbally assaulted by the n-word.

My dark brown hair was in two neatly braided cornrows, weaved by Mama's strong hands. With precise clarity, I can remember what I was wearing, what I was doing, where I was walking to … and that the sun's brightly shining rays weren't strong enough to warm and repair my crushed twelve year old spirit. My pants were royal blue polyester, a cotton blend with a stretch waistband made by Mama on her antique sewing machine purchased from the local church's weekly summer rummage sale in 1994. I had helped her choose it by pointing it out with my little finger, "She looks so lonely in that little dusty dark corner."

As I walked down those halls that morning, I wore my favorite cotton button-up short-sleeve white shirt, painted with vertical multicolored stripes. Until the n-word had penetrated my small mocha colored ears, my morning had started out with a youthful optimism, inspired by my ride on the bus through the warm late summer rural New England ambiance. I had sat in the back of the bus, clutching my new Hello Kitty thermos, while an inviting sun rose from the East, drenching me, and the rolling green hills, with warm love and fresh renewal.

I had exited the bus and felt like a "big kid." No longer was I, Savannah Penelope Sales, in elementary school. I was in middle school. A smile of pride, eagerness and confidence brightened my thin face as I entered through those creaky lobby metal doors and made my way to find my locker number 156. No more desk to put my stuff in. I had a locker!

As I slowly walked past the art department, in a crowded hallway of high school kids, a young male's voice echoed, "Look at that skinny little nigger."—

—That sound! That unforgettable miserable sound had startled, shocked, and appalled me. Less than the time it takes for a hummingbird to flutter a tiny wing, my smile had been replaced by a trembling lower lip. My chest had tightened and my stomach immediately twisted and turned. I had thought that I would not be able to control my bowels before making it to the closest bathroom. I remember I had nervously turned around to see who had said it. Unfortunately, the halls were crowded and the coward had strategically hidden within a sea of white adolescent faces with chattering mouths. He had to have been referring to me, for I had been the only Black girl in that ocean of whiteness.

My calm saunter had become a quick-paced and terror-stricken gait. Tear-filled eyes focused on making it through the double doors that partitioned the high school from the middle school. Like clockwork, the coward stung again, "Run skinny little nigger, run." A sadistic cackle had trailed after his vicious utterance. As I had hurried through the double doors, I remember my small heart had been beating furiously through my chest. It had become increasingly difficult for me to breath and even harder to prevent the tears in my eyes from escaping down my soft cheeks. I remember commanding myself not to have an asthma attack. Foolishly thinking I was "too old" for my inhaler, I had left it underneath my pillow earlier that morning.

"Run skinny little nigger, run," kept on echoing in my head. Would he take the next step and follow me through those doors? What would he do to me? I'm barely five feet tall, what if he's really big? What if no one will help me?

Undeniably, the n-word is the worst word in the English language. He had known this, which is why he had been unable to fire it to my face. Seven years later, I have always wondered why none of my schoolmates had heard it. Maybe they had but it simply didn't incite the petrified terror in them that it did in me. As soon as his vocal cords clamored "nigger" at my back, it instantly connected me to America's sordidly violent and racist past. My mind had begun to rapidly fire through a memory bank of collective misery: faded photographs of lynched Black bodies surrounded by sadistic grimacing white-faced onlookers; Norman Rockwell's unforgettable little Black angel in *The Problem We All Live With;* *Life* magazine's portraits of Black people being hosed down and chewed upon by German Shepherd dogs; Langston Hughes' *Black Misery*; and lastly, the memory of my mama pounding her fist on our kitchen table before I departed for my first day of Kindergarten, "Never let anyone call you a 'nigger.' Do you hear me, Savi? You beat that idea out of them if they do." By the third grade, Mama had made sure that I knew about my people. Our people. The bookcases of our living room were filled with any books and articles about us that she could

3

get her hands on: Toni Morrison's *Beloved*, August Wilson's *The Piano Lesson*, and Ntozake Shange's *For Colored Girls Who Have Considered Suicide When the Rainbow is Enuf* to name a few.

Of course my schoolmates had not been terrified of that word. Their whiteness was their security clearance, a pass to a collective amnesia that blessed them with only happy memories of America's "patriotic textbook." I learned immediately that a fair-skinned Jesus and God were protecting them and only them. Their whiteness was my insecurity coupled with the fact that I was the "token" Black girl in our predominantly white blue-collar town.

Most Black people in America have been or will eventually be called the n-word. However, it doesn't make my story any less significant. It's not just a word in the English language.

Sticks and stones ... When I was eight, I broke my arm when my bicycle collided into a slow moving car at the intersection near my home ... *may break my bones* ...

Bones break. They hurt. They heal. However ... *but words will never hurt me* ...

"Nigger" hurts, scars ...

... and never heals.

NOTES

[i] Cullen, Countee in *Anthology of Modern American Poetry*. Cary Nelson (Ed.). New York City: Oxford University Press, 2007. Page 530.

PART I: DIS-PACED, DIS-LOCATED

...odydeadbodiesmurderedbodiesimportedbredmutilatedbodiessoldb
odiesboughttheEuropeantrafficinbodiesthattellingsomuchaboutthema
nandwhichhelpingfueltheindustrializationofthemetropolisesbodiesbo
diescreatingwealththecapitalfeedingtheindustrialrevolutionsmanytime
soverandoverandoverthebodies...

Between the legs   thespace
/with the womb   thespace
colonized like place and space

thesilenceof
thespacebetween
    the legs

thesilenceof
thespacewithin
    the womb ...

—Marlene Nourbese Philip
"Dis Place"[ii]

NOTES

[ii] Cited from McKittrick, Katherine (2006). *Demonic grounds: Black women and the cartographies of struggle* (p. 48). Minneapolis: University of Minnesota Press.

CHAPTER ONE

1993

Pieces of biscuit-brown cocoa butter slowly melt on top of my ashy bruised knees.

As I squirm a bit between the warm confines of Mama's legs she says "I don't understand these little kids. Why do they push my baby around like that? It's kindergarten for god's sake!" We are both silent for about a minute; the only sound I can hear are the three cows mooing across the street from us. I named them Twinkle, Sandy, and Princess. They live inside of a fenced off area right next to Mr. Danielson's tiny blue painted barn that had fallen down last summer. Mama says that Mr. Danielson's sons are too cheap to help him fix it. Sometimes I wish we could live there. Mr. Danielson has lots and lots of land with maple trees. They are my favorite! And I really love that tiny pond with those white ducks.

"Stop moving, please!" she says, pulling the bushy hair on my head, trying to ease it into neat little cornrows. I am wearing the turquoise sequin dress that Mama bought last week. My warm bottom presses against the cool linoleum floor. Mama reaches into the jar of blue greasy goo on the chair beside me. Her fingers pull out a lump of glistening teal. It shimmers slightly underneath the sixty-watt bulb in our dimly lit kitchen.

"Damn, you have the driest scalp. These New England winters sure can leave a negro so ashy!" Mama exclaims, gently rubbing the goo onto my scalp. As a portion of my itchy skin finds salvation under Mama's smooth fingertips, I giggle in relief. For a few seconds, I forget about being pushed into the pavement by Teresa Bateman, earlier that day.

"I don't know why they always push my baby around," she says again. I grab the scratched leg of the wooden chair beside me, and start playing with a shiny screw that Davis' daddy had put in last month to fix it.

"Savannah! Please stop moving so much! This ain't going to make it go faster. Why'd you let that little girl push you like that? Stop moving!" she warns, weaving my hair into one of her unique patterns. This time she said she'd make a spiral on each side of the part on my head. I hope she doesn't pull them too tightly. I can never sleep good the first night she does it. Last month I couldn't even close my eyes, she had braided them so tightly. Mama's braids were destined to never unravel from my rowdy head.

I reach forward to scratch my tender knee, but before my bitten down fingernails can touch it, Mama says, "If you keep on scratching them they are going to never heal and then they are going to fall off. You know how stupid you're going to look wit' no knees? You be a no knee Negro." My right arm retracts instantly as I try not to envision myself walking to school with no knees. Is that possible?

"Is that too tight?" she asks, as I feel her finishing up the last row. I nod eagerly, hoping she'll unravel them all and start over again, perhaps showing more mercy to my scalp.

"Well, why didn't you say something before, Savi?"

"I don't know."

"Well, they'll loosen up in a day or two. Now, stand up so I can look at you. I want to make sure they're goin' in the right direction so your head don't look crooked," she says with a giggle. I giggle back with, "Come on, Mama! Do it! Do it!" I raise my arms up in the air. Her strong arms and hands swing me to my feet like she always does. Whirling me around to face her, I whisper, "Is my head crooked?" She cocks her head slightly sideways and grimaces, "Nope, not anymore. Just tell the kids to look at you like this." She cocks her head even more to the side then crosses her eyes.

"Mama!" She tickles me in my belly for a few seconds then squats down and gives me a hug, "I love my crooked headed little princess." Her body and scent engulf me as my nostrils fill with the mélange of fragrances from Mama's blouse: Virginia Slims, Secret deodorant, Crisco cooking oil and a hint of Bounce fabric softener.

She sits back down on the kitchen chair with me on her lap.

"Mama, what's a L.A. riot?"

"Why you wanna know that?" she asks with curious eyes. Looking down at her shirt, I start playing with a purple button and then shrug with a small whisper, "Because I want to know."

"Well, a bunch of Negroes actin' foolish. That's what the L.A. riots are. They're pissed off for the right reasons but now they just actin' foolish. Burnin' up they own communities. Foolishness. 'Should be burnin' up some rich white folks' houses instead."

"Well, Teresa said—well, she said—"

"That little white girl who pushed you today? What did that little girl say?"

"Well—"

"Look up at me when you talking, poopie bear. Always look people in the eyes when you are talking to them—even grown folk." I lift up my tightly braided head, and then nervously peer into Mama's captivating and serious eyes.

"She said her daddy says that Black people are crazy animals and that's why there's a L.A. riot—"

"Oh!? So those four white folk aren't crazy animals for beating the piss out of that poor man?" I shrug, not knowing who she's talking about.

"She said that we were animals Mama. I told her that she was stupid and then she pushed me." Securing me with one arm, she reaches across the table and grabs the phone book.

"What's her last name?"

"Bateman." Within several seconds, she has found the phone number. Finger on the page, squinting her eyes, she mumbles, "Let's give a J. L. Bateman a 'wake-up' call. Gimme the phone baby." I tentatively slide off of her lap, then amble towards the phone on the kitchen counter and bring it to her.

"You want to sit back on my lap?" I shake my head nervously and then sit across from her. Calmly, she lifts up the receiver and dials the number. As I hold my breath, I can faintly hear the phone ringing on the other end.

"Hello?" I barely hear on the other end. Mama perks up.

"Is this the J. L. Bateman residence..? OK, is this Mr. Bateman who has a little girl named Teresa? Because I want to make sure I got the right place ...?" I begin chewing the inside of my cheeks, worried what Teresa will do to me at school tomorrow.

"... For what? Because I got an important message for you and your daughter Mr. J. L. Bateman ..." she quickly takes the phone from her ear and stares directly at the receiver, "Fuck you and your

Nazi ass daughter!" The phone slams down and I jump up, startled. My tiny body is numb. Do I cry or do I laugh?

Mama reaches into her shirt pocket and pulls out one Virginia Slims cigarette. Squinting my eyes disapprovingly, I vividly remember that yesterday she had vowed to quit because it worsened both our asthma and the cough she has had for the past year.

"It's shit like this that makes it hard to quit." Sighing and shaking her head, she lights it, stands up, and leaves our dimly lit apartment.

CHAPTER TWO

February 4, 2007
11:57 A.M.

Dear Diary,

I had the dream again. Same damn dream for three years now. Seems like that's all these pages are ever filled with. Though his face is blurry, I know it is him … His body is nearly ghostly white, his teeth are sharp ivory razors, and several long sharp red-hot daggers have replaced his genitalia. This time, I am a toddler and crying—screaming at the top of my lungs, unable to move. As usual, everything in the nightmare is always fragmented. One moment Mama isn't there and the next moment she appears out of nowhere, trying to run away from him. But he always catches her and throws her down, violently onto the floor … then I forget what happens. Every time I have awakened from that nightmare, the end of the dream fades away upon my reentry into the conscious world.

Earlier this morning, I woke up sobbing but with no memory of the end of the dream. Why can't I ever remember? As usual, my body remembers. Last time, I found myself rushing into our small bathroom to puke my brains out. For some strange reason, the thought of carrot cake cupcakes enters my mind and makes my stomach howl.

I spent the rest of the night in the bathroom, afraid to fall back to sleep, trying to calm my nerves. I know hot baths are a lot of money, but I really needed one. I'll work extra hours to pay for the hot water bill. I swear, my heart was still beating so fast, I could see the surface of the water trembling around me.

I know I shouldn't be thinking about this, but I think about it all the time. I saw the pink Gillette razor at the edge of the bathtub and contemplated doing more than just shaving my slim legs with it. I know I shouldn't be writing this.

These are the mental atrocities I have always kept to myself, along with other fragments of my identity that are archived in my most top secret war trenches; so deep that maybe I should be calling

11

them war abysses. They remain there because this conglomerate of psychological shrapnel scares the hell out of me. I have never told Mama about those nightmares about him. She did what she did to save us and didn't need me telling her that it has caused these nightmares. Mama has to think that I'm fine and has to believe that I think the space between her legs has never known pain.

***

My red Hello Kitty alarm clock buzzes at full volume. I hit the off-button so it doesn't wake up Mama. Turning, I see her face buried in the pillow, hands over her head, pressing her face deeper into the pillow. She had fallen asleep beside me last night, while we were talking. I must have been completely knocked out. I didn't even realize she hadn't gone to her own room.

"Sorry," I whisper to her. She mumbles something into the pillow, then removes her face, turns onto her back, yawns, scratches the scalp under her short afro, then pulls the sunburst orange and teal colored down comforter over her head.

Same drill every day, I think, rolling out of bed.

5:00 a.m. Another cold winter day. The bedroom is cold and biting, as usual. I look at my March 2007 Hello Kitty calendar image of the month. Well, spring is right around the corner. It won't be too cold for too much longer. Sitting at the edge of the bed, I rub my eyes, sniff, and try not to think about my shift at Quikstop. Maybe today will be different.

As usual I fight the urge to just say 'Screw it and screw all of them,' and roll back into bed. When was the last time I slept past five? I cannot remember. Sighing, I stand up. The cold air in the room envelopes me and I shiver.

Some people want long vacations in Europe, others, a brand new car. All I want is to wake up in the morning and not freeze to death. Rubbing my nose, I think, it's such a simple request. Not selfish ... And I know this ain't good for Mama—

I suddenly interrupt my own thoughts, not wanting to think about that 'unwanted house guest' so early in the morning. It will just make the day harder to get through. Several minutes later, I am eating a bowl of hot oatmeal, mixed with fake blueberries. I am trying my damnedest to start and finish my homework before my shift starts at seven.

My assignment is comical and offensive. Sniffing, I shake my head as I read the first page, Social Theories of Poverty. When I first enrolled into the class, I thought my decision had been a colossal mistake. During the first week, all we read was literature written by snobby white dudes with graduate degrees from all prestigiously white snobby institutions. As a freshman, I thought college would be different from the K-12 Eurocentric B.S.

"What do they know about poverty? About working your butt off for low pay? Theory! I am not a 'theoretical' person. I'm a real goddamn poor person," I wanted to yell during our first class meeting. However, I didn't have enough confidence to say how I felt because I wasn't sure how Professor Rogards would take it, that first day of class. Would he be just like my teachers in elementary, middle, and high schools? My K-12 teachers never brought the color question into the literature we would read for English class; nor did my classmates raise the question, except for 'Nigger Jim,' who passed through our reading assignment. God, how I loathed every instance of that word within the pages of that timeless American classic. I'll never forget the day we had our eighth grade class discussion about the book, when most of us had to read excerpts out loud. When it was my turn, and I had to say 'nigger' in front of Jim's name, I replaced it with 'brother.' Ms. Ruport told me that I could not do that while the class giggled. She said to me, in the most condescending tone, "You don't have to say the n-word. I understand, but seriously, no one uses that word anymore anyway, so you shouldn't let it bother you because it's a thing of the past."

I turn the book over and there is the author's picture. As expected, he is a middle-aged white man in a scholarly setting with a plethora of books in chestnut colored bookcases that we are to have assumed he has read. Reading aloud, "Shelby Wilson Stevens, born in Westport, Connecticut, graduated from Princeton University— of course—in 1952." In a snobby snooty voice, I pretend to be Shelby, "Let me tell you what poverty is all about while I spend a year sabbatical in the Bahamas to write this pathetic excuse for scholarship." To an empty kitchen, I exclaim, "They should have me school them in this stuff. I got nineteen years of experience that their PhDs can't even touch!"

"Savannah, shut up! Jesus, I'm trying to sleep. What are you making all that noise for?" I hear Mama interrupt from the bedroom. I fall off my soapbox and plunge back into the reality of our small kitchen. My ego bounces off the edge of the table then shatters onto the sage and blue-checkered linoleum floor.

"Sorry, Mama!"

Looking at the clock on the stove, I realize that I have roughly one hour and thirty minutes to speed read this B.S. perception of poverty. Sighing, I take one last gulp of my fake blueberry oatmeal and take the plunge into the mind of yet another egotistical intellectual masturbator with a penis and fair skin …

***

Welcome to East Lebanon, Connecticut, my hometown.

Whenever Davis and I are driving back to East Lebanon, we are greeted by a wooden sign that states when the town was "settled." Once in a while I propose to Davis that I should consider adjusting this historical inaccuracy and post my own greeting juxtaposed to it: "Taken from indigenous people and made into an African slave trade distribution point for free landowning white men." Davis responds with a long sigh, rolls his eyes, then usually tells me to stop being bitter and to "stop living in the past." Of course he says that. He and his family came from the original East Lebanon settlers, supposedly emigrating from an oppressive British Empire. He wouldn't understand.

Almost nineteen years old and I've lived in East Lebanon for nearly eighteen of them. A small, once thriving agricultural town, East Lebanon is the home to about seven thousand people. Mama and I are among a few handfuls of folks that make up that .5% of "people of color" statistic in the town's census. Though Mama was born in Georgia, Mama refuses to tell me why she decided to hop on the bus in Georgia, nearly nine months pregnant with me, and move her life to Connecticut. "When you're old enough, I will tell you what you need to know," she used to always say. Even worse, whenever I would ask more about my father, she'd tell me, "You really don't need to worry about that, ya hear?" What could I do in response other than sit in complacent anger as my peers spoke of their fathers?

For nearly two decades we've managed to remain here. Us two poor Black girls with Seminole and African blood running through our veins. Part of Mama's enigmatic history had involved an 'arrangement' made with the son of the landlord's nearly two decades ago. My imagination still sparkles with curiosity as I try to envision Mama, in 1989, arriving in an all white town with a tattered eleven-month-old baby girl in tow.

I don't know why or what circumstances led to it, but from the time of my birth until the 'arrangement,' Mama tells me that she had ended up homeless in Hartford, Connecticut, by way of a one-way bus ticket from Georgia. When she arrived in Hartford, she says she was nearly nine months pregnant and gave birth to me two days later. The details are murky, but we apparently lived in various shelters and halfway homes for teenagers, after I was born.

When Mama was in the middle of finding another shelter for us, she met some old white guy named Scott. She had been sitting with me at a bus stop during a winter storm. We had been without shelter and enduring torrential rain and ice storms for several days. She never told me this, but I pretty much pieced together her story from eavesdropping in on conversations she has had, with Mr. and Mrs. Allen, off and on, throughout the years. Maybe I put the puzzle together wrong and my conclusions are wrong. However, at a very early age, I quickly grasped the idea of America being a land of many wolves, many sheep, and only a handful of shepherds that are usually outnumbered by the helplessness of the sheep and the merciless nature of the wolves. I no longer need her to give me the specific story. She was nineteen, hungry and cold with a baby who was becoming sick from exposure. Through my eavesdropping, I have concluded that Scott was the son of our first landlords.

She was alone.

She was cold and hungry with a sickly baby girl.

Every time I try not to think of this story, I cringe and collapse into a state of lamentation and tears. The nightmares I have been having for the last three years tell me that Scott used her body as currency. Mama has told me that she got this apartment through a 'special arrangement': a secret between she and Scott. My mind screams against this image of Scott and Mama that I have burned into my head and recent nightmares from the past three years: It is 1989 and I am ten months old. I am in the living room of the apartment that will soon become my future home. I am crying in the living room. In the bedroom, behind closed doors, my mother's spirit is finally broken, over and over again, as she makes untraceable payments to Scott with her body. At that defining moment that makes us who we are truly meant to be, my mind tells me that he chose to be a wolf over the shepherd, and rip apart the very vessel that gave birth to me—my sanctuary. I know that this is why she tells me that it is a secret. Who would want their daughter to know this about their mother?

No, she doesn't have to tell me that this happened. He was a white man and it was 1989. What else could have happened? What else could that 'special arrangement' have entailed?

A year or two later, the landlords sold their properties and retired to Arizona.

In 2B, second floor, life's wounds have transformed into ugly scars; loathsome scars that manifest into emotional breakdowns, ulcers, blind rages … and Mama's emphysema; the "unwanted house guest."

2B, second floor has a distant view of the Quikstop store half a mile away, engulfed by sprawling green hills. It's the apartment I've grown to call home, to love … and to hate.

CHAPTER THREE

"The radio is too loud. Can you turn it down?" A wiry forty-something year old woman with yellow teeth asks, as she digs into her ear with her left index finger. She is holding a bag of pretzels and a boxed douche. She comes here several times a month, always buying a Massengil or tampons. Like I need to know the most recent status of what's going on in between her legs.

"Yes m'am," I reply, pretending to be a cheerful shuffling Negro. *Loser, why do you care? You don't have to stay here forever, like me.* Sighing, I look at my watch, "Only eight forty-five." *I hate this place. If I have to work here one more month, I am going to kill all the customers and then myself—*

"Excuse me, I'm talking to you," a rather annoying husky male voice interrupts. I lift my head up to the presence of a fat balding white man wearing a sleeveless tee shirt and yellow worn-out sweat pants, "Yes, sir?" Yes sir, Master Charlie. Super Negro at your service!

"Ten dollars on pump two."

"Did you pump already or will you be pumping?"

"I haven't pumped yet, obviously," he answers, overemphasizing the 'obviously' through gritted teeth and parsed lips. If I kill him, will anyone miss him? I want to sneer at him, "Die you jackass, die." But God forbid if I ever said this to any of them. I am not allowed to tell the world to stop using Mama and me as their personal toilet bowls. Not only am I supposed to take it, I am supposed to take it with bright eyes and a smile, because that is what servants do. Ask anyone to describe what a 'shit-eating grin' looks like and they'll show you a snapshot of my face as I cater to *their* needs and demands for service.

Several minutes later, old bald fatty has left and I continue sitting behind the register on the butt numbing wooden stool. As usual, my right leg has fallen asleep. I poke at it and am greeted with the familiar sensation of pins and needles. I should be reading that stupid Shelby book before class starts ... but it's so boring.

"Young lady, can you please turn the radio down?" The same lady asks again.

"I did," I lie. I poke at my sleeping limb. More pins and needles.

"Well, could you turn it down some more? I can't think about what I am going to buy. Thank you."

"It's not that loud," I whisper. The bell to the entrance door jingles. I don't bother paying any attention to who comes in this time. I guess I should in case it's a third rate robber ready to end my miserable existence by blowing out my under-appreciated brains with his sawed-off shotgun for less than three hundred bucks in the register. Dumb ass probably doesn't know that practically everyone pays with plastic here 'cause they're always too broke ass to have actual cash on them.

"Savannah Boo Bear!" It is not a dumb ass third-rate robber. I look up at the familiar voice of my best friend, Davis Allen. He is wearing the puke gray sweater I knitted for him last winter. Only a true friend would wear such a project-gone-wrong. I knitted the collar too big and the left sleeve is three inches longer than the right.

Leaning over the counter, I give him a hug. Fragrances of Old Spice after-shave, *Enoz* moth balls, and sandalwood cologne fill my nostrils. It is his signature scent that can fill any room. As usual, he is smiling brightly, holding a cup of mocha coffee in his left hand with no sugar but plenty of cream; gastric-intestinal death to the stomachs of us lactose intolerant people.

Looking directly at him, I roll my big light brown eyes and sign, "Guess what lady keeps on complaining about how loud she thinks the music is?" Putting his coffee down, he signs, "Let me guess … 'Tampon Queen' again?" I grin, "Close. Today she's decided on the douche," I sign back. He makes a squeamish face then leans over the counter and whispers into my ear, "Tell her I said she must be nuts because I can't hear anything," looks down my thin silk woven V-neck sweater and continues, "Oh, is that a black lace bra?" I push him away and frown at him for several seconds. He gives me a cute boyish 'I'm innocent' facial expression then mouths, "I'm sorry. They were just there!"

Till this day, I still don't understand how anyone can read lips as well as Davis. I often wonder if he is a mind reader or simply a brilliant boy who has tackled losing his hearing at the age of two, by learning how to read lips at an "X-Men super power" level. He rarely fails to understand me except when I am drunk and have forgotten what articulation and enunciation are.

"Don't you have something to do? You're always bothering me. Some of us do work, you know?" I sign with a smile.

"I have a job, you know?"

"Teaching little kids Sign, six hours a day at Stonehill, is not a real job. You know all you do is play with them."

"Hater."

"You're a babysitter," I sign.

"Whatever. I've told you once, I've told you twice: There are two job openings for people who can sign and enjoy working with children."

"I hate kids," I reply, shaking my head, "You know I hate kids."

"But you hate working here too. What do you want, then?" I reply with a roll of my eyes and a sigh of annoyance.

"Stop sulking and complaining then." I give him a 'whatever' facial expression. He grabs his coffee cup and says, "Anyway, I gotta get to work—"

"Right now? What about class? I have class, remember?"

"I have to help Liz update the web page for the kids, and she wants it done by the end of the week. Violet's has faster Wi-Fi now, so I'll be there. It'll only take a few hours. Don't worry; I will be back in time to pick up your ungrateful butt." He reaches over and pinches my cheek like he always seems compelled to do, "They're not as plump as they used to be. Are you losing weight? You know you're hot just the way you are."

"Be quiet," I sign.

"Smile. You're scaring the customers," he says with a giggle. Several seconds later, my best friend is gone, walking towards his twenty year old hatchback mini Cooper clunker of a car.

Drawing the collar of my sweater to my nose, I sniff. Within a microsecond, I am grinning at the aromatic remnants of cologne and after-shave that Davis has left behind. *What the hell am I going to do when he leaves for college this fall? First Esperanza and now Davis.*

As I think about life without Davis, I notice that the fifty-something year old white man wearing a Red Sox baseball cap, who entered the store twenty minutes ago, is still here. He is on the other side, perusing the magazines on the cold metal display racks. Though I have never seen him before, I immediately feel that I do not like him. Finally, he chooses a magazine, turns around, licks and sucks his lips quietly, grins, then slowly approaches the register. As he drifts towards me, new Converse sneakers squeaking on the linoleum, I feel what can only be described as a chill of fear seizing my brown skin. Before he can get to the register, my arms command me to hide my body and my D size breasts. As fast as I can, I am grabbing my winter coat and zipping it up to my neck.

He arrives at the counter. In his left hand is the porn magazine, Wo!Man. Methodically, he looks at the magazine, looks at me, looks down at the magazine again, then ultimately places it onto the countertop and then slides it towards me; a slimy grin on his chalky face. Instantaneously, the comforting scent of Davis has died and is replaced by the redolence of a sweating beast. Slowly creeping from the bottom of my hungry stomach, I am overwhelmed with the sensation of being like a fox that has been cornered by hounds; by white men on their stately white horses on some plantation from the 1700s.

"You didn't have to do that," he starts, his conniving grin refusing to leave his face. I respond with crumpled eyebrows and a shaky customer friendly half-smile, "I'm sorry—what?" Just pay and leave. Just freaking pay and leave!

I quickly scan the store and realize that he and I are the only ones present. Why does Kitter sell this garbage here? It just attracts the freaky Chester the Molester types.

"A pretty little thing like yourself shouldn't hide under that winter coat," he continues. Fervently, I ignore the comment then ask him, "Is this it?" and avoid looking at the picture on the cover of Wo!Man.

"Foxy ladies, huh?" he says, pointing to the cover. I refuse to look, and then repeat, with a nervous customer friendly smile, "Is this it?" I place my left hand on top of the magazine, hiding the cover woman's face and torso. I take the scanner from the register and move my small hand that is on top of the magazine, slightly to the right. I scan the bar code while not allowing my eyes to gaze at what his eyes have been visually consuming.

As the picture of the cover girl's legs dangle beneath my hand, I notice that they are brown, nearly the same tone as mine. I have seen the cover women on these magazines when restocking the display shelves every month. It is rare that I see brown or black legs "grace" its cover. Below her legs is the title, "The Blacker the Berry …"

"So, East Lebanon doesn't have no exotic ladies like that, so I don't know if it's true."

"That'll be eight bucks," I respond, refusing to make eye contact with him.

"That's pretty expensive. These ladies always are …" With my peripheral vision, I see him reaching into his back pocket for his money, "… but, can't say I wouldn't pay a lot more for the real thing," he says with an insidious cackle, pretending that he is halfheartedly joking.

"Eight bucks, huh? That's probably more than they give you people per hour here, huh? That's a shame. Pretty little thing like yourself deserves more," then puts a crisp fifty-dollar bill on the side of the magazine.

"Sorry sweetie, I just cashed my check and I always ask for it in fifties. This isn't too big for you, is it?"

"Nope," I quickly reply, grabbing the fifty, then punching the amount into the register with my furious and scared fingers. I try to place his change back onto the spot where he had left the bill for me to take. My attempt to not be touched by him fails. His pudgy fish belly white hands quickly grasp then slide the money out of my hand. In measurement of time, I know it is a quick and brief action, but it is a short moment that feels and last longer than I want it to. I feel warm sweat and an aggressive firmness as his calloused hands intentionally graze the top and bottom of my frigid hand …

… the pit of my stomach twists and burns as I vomit into the employee toilet bowl. I cannot stop visualizing Scott on top of my mother, tearing into her. As I wretch again, the searing face of Scott mutates into him and my mother's agonizing face turns into mine.

2007 and they still sell trash like that. Blacker the Berry! BLACKER THE BERRY!!!??? I vomit the last bits of this anger from my body then pull myself up by the edge of steel sink. Immediately, I turn the hot water on, pump a large amount of antibacterial soap onto my hand, and then furiously start washing the hand he had touched. A cracked mirror hangs in front of me, but I cannot look at it. I cannot look at myself right now.

The scolding water burns, helping to move the anguish from those burning images of Scott and mama in my head, onto my hands. The nerves underneath the brown smoothness of my skin scream to my brain to be relieved, but I do not remove it. My mind screams back in retaliation, *Why did you let him touch your hand—touch you!? Why did you let him get away with that!?*

***

1997

I am reading a book that my mother has bought me as a gift. It is the evening of my ninth birthday and she and I are in bed. I love how we read a new book about Black people once a week.

I am sitting in between her legs, holding the book and reading to her. It is *To Be Young, Gifted and Black*, by some lady named Lorraine Hansberry. I do not know who she is. I do not understand most of what I have read. Mama keeps on telling me that it's because I'm too young but that it's important for me to know about folk like myself; that she remembered seeing the play "A Raisin in the Sun," when she was seventeen years old. She said she had never been much of a reader, but seeing that play had always made her regret that she hadn't read more stuff by our people much earlier in her life.

I have been reading in bed for the past hour, struggling with the hard words but pushing on because I can feel Mama's pride as her arms squeeze me tightly, every time I make it through a hard word. She says, "Good baby," followed by a soft kiss right on the perfectly lined part on my scalp that separates my two glistening brown cornrows from one another.

I am yawning as I start page ninety-eight. I am almost on page one hundred and this excites me! It is the longest book I have ever read! Over two hundred pages long and very few pictures! Wait until I tell Davis!

Mama intervenes as she notices me yawn, "Baby boo, if you are tired, we can go to sleep."

"No, Mama. I want to get to page one hundred," I whisper, sleepy from a fun-filled birthday party playing with Davis and eating too much chicken and cake.

"Okay, you continue then," she says with approval. My small hands clasping the pages, I continue, "Light up on first Black woman, a young doo—domestic worker ... Young Woman. All right. So now you know something 'bout me you didn't know! In these streets out there, any little white boy from Long Is—" I catch myself from saying 'is,' always forgetting that the 's' in island is silent. I continue, "... Island or West—Westchester sees me and leans out of his car and yells—, 'Hey there, hot chocolate! Say there, Jez—Jez ... Jezebel!'" I pause then turn my neck towards Mama and ask, "Like in the Bible?" She nods. I continue, "Hey you—'Hundred Dollar Misunderstanding!' YOU! Bet you know where there's a good time tonight.' Follow me sometimes and see if I lie. I can be coming from eight hours on an assembly line or fourteen hours in Mrs. Hal—Halsey's kitchen. I can be all filled up that day with three hundred years of rage so that my eyes are flashing and my flesh is trembling and the white boys in the streets, they look at me and think of sex—" I stop, trying not be embarrassed. It is the first book I've ever read that has the word 'sex' in it.

"Keep on reading, it's okay. Nothing to be ashamed of," Mama whispers.

"OK, Mama ... 'They look at me and that's all they think ... Baby, you could be Jesus in drag—but if you're brown they're sure you're selling!'"

I look up at Mama, confused. She doesn't say anything for about a minute. But then, she tells me to close the book, wraps her arms around me and begins to cry.

I do not understand ...

CHAPTER FOUR

"Savannah, come on!" Erick says to me. I clear my throat and the classroom is suddenly quiet. My peers wait for me to continue my argument with Erick about Shelby Wilson Stevens' lame-ass theories of why people end up in a never-ending cycle of poverty. As usual, I am in conflict with Erick, the token privileged white boy from Weston, Massachusetts, attending a community college filled with working class people. You do the math.

"Stevens is not saying anything new. Not only is he playing the age old game of blaming the victim of poverty for their social class—"

"Oh please!" Erick interrupts.

"She's still talking, Erick," Professor Rogards tells Erick. Erick sighs, rolls his eyes and I continue, "This book is about poverty in the city. NYC is his case study. He uses statistics and interviews of Latinos and Blacks. Then, he selects his rural community case study as a small town in Alabama—and no less, a poor Black community. He is falling into the stereotype that poverty can only exist in the rural south or urban city of NYC or Detroit or L.A. Those are major well known densely populated areas and he speaks of the Latino and Black population again—"

"Savannah, his statistics are accurate, though," Lee Voight tells me.

"People are not statistics, Lee," my classmate, Joan Li, pipes up. She winks at me for me to continue delivering my point.

"Everyone already knows this. I know this book was written twenty-five years ago and considered to be a 'classic,' but he ain't telling us anything innovative, creative, or helpful. I know we're supposed to understand that this book was pivotal in influencing the government officials to introduce new anti-poverty legislation, but his book probably caused more damage than good."

"How is that possible? He's an emeritus at Princeton University; so obviously, someone thinks he knows what he's talking about," Erick asks.

"Well, Mr. Erick ... Poverty is often equated with Latinos and Blacks in either the rural South or East and West Coast cities.

But what about Appalachia? Not only are people living below the poverty line, it is rural and a majority of the people are white. What about right here in Southeastern Connecticut? There are people who live in poverty or close to it in my hometown of East Lebanon and it is rural and ninety-nine percent white. Maybe Shelby doesn't have problems blaming Blacks and Latinos for being poor—"

"He doesn't blame them, Savannah," Erick interrupts.

"Read between the lines, Erick," Joan Li blurts, opening the text then reading from her book, "Look right here, page thirty-eight, and second paragraph." Half the class picks up their texts and turns to the page. Joan continues, "The only time he ever brings up white people is when he says, 'Many whites plunged into poverty because their jobs were in factories that took significant wage cuts during the 1960s. Many whites decided to quit in order to find better opportunities to support their families. However, once they realized that there were no immediate jobs in other surrounding industrial towns, they returned to their previous employer, hoping to work there again, even if it meant at lower wages. Little did they know, Negroes—And who says Negroes anymore?—and Puerto Ricans had replaced them. Unlike whites, these new workers had no problem working for poverty-level wages and living in poverty stricken ghettos.'"

"How is that racist, Joan?" Lee asks.

"He's merely stating a factual point he concluded after four years of field research," Erick says in defense of this emeritus professor.

I shake my head furiously, "No, no, no! He's implying that brown and Black people have 'no problem' living and working in poverty. You can't get any more crystal clear racist than that! He's also generalizing an entire people."

"Savannah, it's obvious he's generalizing," Erick exclaims.

"That's a problem," June Wilson says to Erick. June's cool for a white girl. She grew up homeless until she was twelve, so she gets it.

"Stevens can't include all groups. No theorists can represent everything. Automatically, something has to be eliminated for the theory to work," Erick argues.

"Then it doesn't really work and it ain't—"

"—Isn't" Erick corrects me.

"—Whatever—ain't conducive to a reality of six billion perspectives, identities and experiences that are more than just fun subject matter for his grant funded research," I explain to Erick. Professor Rogards turns toward me with curiosity, his bushy gray eyebrows raised up high. Damn he looks like that wizard dude from Lord of the Rings.

"Then what do you propose Stevens should have done differently, when embarking on his research, Ms. Sales?"

"It's not that the book is one hundred percent inaccurate. I know it was written before I was born and I know this is a survey class, so we're reading all different perspectives on social welfare studies. My problem is that he writes that his theories are objective and neutral and claims that his approach is universal and can be applied to the basis of how to understand poverty in America," I spout out in one breath.

"Remember to breathe girl!" Joan exclaims. The class laughs and I continue, "You can't use one theory so generally. Poverty is too complex. Therefore, he should include in his introduction the groups he is marginalizing and why. He should tell us why he has pursued 'social welfare' studies as a white privileged dude. What are his goals? Is he doing this to help those living in poverty or is it all about being published and remaining in his cushy office, grant funded by an ivory tower that has never existed in the ghetto? His mistake is that he assumes his theory is consistent throughout America—and he totally forgets about other groups like Native Americans ... And what about Asians?"

"Asians aren't poor," Lois Green comments. I roll my eyes and Rogards grins.

"Hello, what planet are you on, Lois?" Joan asks.

"Well, they aren't. Stevens didn't include them because they are a model minority. Do you ever see any homeless Asians in the city?" Lois exclaims.

"My family—we're Vietnamese—and we work our asses off and believe me we are still poor," Joan tells Lois. Lois replies with a blank stare. I smirk at her then look at Joan and mouth, "Right on."

As I collect my books and toss them into my bag, my peripheral visions see Erick moving towards me.

"Lois, hold your rebuttal. We have to finish this debate next week," Professor Rogards says, looking at his watch.

"What rebuttal?" I hear Joan sarcastically whisper to herself.

"Savannah, why can't you just look at theory from a more objective point of view, for once? You shouldn't bring race into everything we read," Erick tells me. Ms. Ruport's words from five years ago, echo in my head, "... *so you shouldn't let it bother you because it's a thing of the past.*" I wonder if I should waste my time responding to him. We have yet to see eye to eye and I doubt we ever will.

"You're middle class, a man, and you're white. I understand why race and class may not be part of your everyday thoughts on social affairs of us poor brown and Black people who make your coffee, clean your toilets, and change your offspring's diapers."

"Whoa, hold up! You don't know anything about me. I only see you in class. You're judging me because of my skin color? Now *that's* racist!" Sighing and rolling my eyes, "Erick, I know you aren't poor and probably have never missed a Christmas because it wasn't in your family's budget. You drive a brand new Mini Cooper, bring a two thousand dollar MacBook to class, wear a Raymond Weil watch, have worn at least five different types of shoes to class. Not to mention, your teeth are perfectly straight and white." Squinting his eyes and shaking his head, he basically ignores the significance of what I have just pointed out as I run my tongue across my crooked and off-white teeth.

"That doesn't mean anything. I'm still able to be objective." I sit back down at my desk and clench my fists. There are two things that immediately drop me into blind rage: cigarettes and oblivious white men's confident and overuse of the word 'objective.' The audacity that well-off white folk have to force us to be objective so they don't have to look deeper into the complexity of race and class —and everything else for that matter—in this country! The audacity!

"For fuck's sake, admit that your white privilege oppresses all us people of color, you stupid cracker!"—Okay, I do not say this, but damn, I want to. It is something I have always wanted to scream at him upon the first day of meeting him, when he told the class he had just returned from skiing at Vail, and I asked, "What's that?" His response was a laugh that translated into, "You don't know where Vail is?"

"Erick," I begin with a sigh, "You and I are different. Nothing I say will make you understand how you ain't objective." I bite my lower lip, waiting for him to argue even more, or even correct me again for saying ain't. He does not reply, and I eventually look up to see what is taking him so long. He is looking at me, rather hurt. I wonder if I have genuinely offended him. I wonder if I should care about his feelings. *Do you realize how many times you people have hurt mine and didn't seem to care?*

Closing his eyes, he shakes his head slowly, "You know nothing about me. If I weren't a white guy, you wouldn't be at conflict with everything I say. You wouldn't always be so angry with me."

"Probably—" Oops. It is supposed to be a thought but it had escaped from my brain and unfolded from my tongue.

"Thanks, Savannah. Thanks a lot," he replies, turning around and shaking his head. *Apologize, you idiot—I don't want to. Maybe he'll start thinking—nah, he'll start hating you even more, now—*

"Erick, sorry," I surprise myself by interrupting my own thoughts. He pauses, probably wondering if he should bother turning around or simply continue walking away.

"Oh, what do I care?" I whisper to myself, looking down at the desk, already trying to decide what to think about next. They always hurt my feelings … What do I care about theirs?

"You should understand that not all white people are bad," I hear him say. I look up, as he is now facing me. Scratching his scalp through his blond crew cut and looking at me with eerie blue eyes, I think, I guess this is where I'm supposed to say, "You're absolutely right …" *Whatever. Screw him and the privileged yacht he sailed in on.*

"I don't think all white people are bad," my lips lie.

"Well, during these past seven weeks, it seems to be evident in everything you've said. You might want to come to terms with the fact that you are prejudiced against white people." I crumple my eyebrows and reply, "Fair." He grimaces a bit and then slowly swallows, wondering what he should say next. Instead of responding to me, he simply turns back around, gesturing that he is about leave. Clenching my small fists tightly, I quickly say, "And you need to be straight up with what it means to be a rich white boy in America." I almost end the statement with a 'bitch,' but then remind myself that I can't say these things in class. He sighs and continues walking away. I whisper it for my own edification, "… bitch!"

***

"So you admit this to him by mistake? That's royally messed up, Savi!" Davis exclaims to me, as I recap my latest conflict between Captain America and I.

"I didn't mean to. I could have called him a cracker," I sign. His hazel green eyes make contact with my caramel colored irises. He crumples his brown eyebrows, "But, you didn't … right?"

"I didn't." It is around six in the evening, and Davis and I are at Violet's Café, as usual.

"You are so bad. I mean, are you sure he's just not acting this way because he's rich? I don't act that way. It's a class thing. I mean, all rich people kind of act elitist, you know? It sounds like this guy is trying, though."

"No he isn't. He thinks he is trying, though. I mean how obnoxious is it that he went to Harvard, and now he's taking a class at a community college 'just for the hell of it' because his organization can pay for it?"

Davis shakes his head, "You know what I am going to say."

"I don't hate white people! They hate me!" I sign and nearly yell at the same time.

"You do, Savi! My brethren do not hate you."

"I just can't … tolerate white people with money that refuse … to admit color matters," I sign back rather slowly but passionately.

"I know. We've had this conversation one million times … You're still a racist, though."

"Black people can't be racist."

"What kind of stupidity is that?" he replies, shaking his head.

"I learned that we can be ethnocentric, but it's not the same or as bad as racism."

"Don't you ever get sick of talking about this?" He sips his coffee then clears his throat, "You're a walking contradiction. I mean, how do you explain my family's commitment to your and Mama Sales' welfare. Last time I checked, we were white … and we love you. My mom and dad didn't give a crap that you're Black when we lent you money for your rent just before the new landlords were going to evict you."

He rarely plays that card: the story of how his parents basically "rescued" Mama and me from being homeless again, two years after finding our way to East Lebanon. I don't know the details; I just know that the building was sold to new landlords, our rent increased, and we couldn't make rent and were about to get the boot. Luckily, Mama got a better paying job as an administrative assistant, at the elementary school, and we were able to make do on our own, a few months after that.

"Are you thinking of a witty response or were you simply spacing out?" Davis asks me with a tentative smile. I simply shrug in reply.

"You've been spacing out a lot, lately," he tells me, leaning over and gingerly caressing my right shoulder, "You okay?"

"It's OK … I'm just a little tired and have a lot of things on my mind lately. I know I've been kind of bitchy lately, anyway, so I guess I deserved that—"

"No, you didn't. I'm sorry, Savi."

Someone sitting in back of me begins to cough. I cringe, close my eyes, and try not to think of Mama. Of course I do anyway. Davis puts his hand on top of mine, "Are sure you're okay? Why is your hand so red?"

"I don't know," I lie. I remember when there was a time that I could tell him everything. Opening my eyes, I smile and nod, "Things are chill. I'm just tired." I have yet to tell him that Mama was recently diagnosed with emphysema; that we are struggling with finding good healthcare services since we are confined to crappy health insurance from the crappy public school system. To cut costs, full-time staff and teachers are given premium health insurance.

Since Mama's position is thirty-two hours per week ("conveniently" three hours short of full time), she qualified for the crappy alternative insurance for employees that do not work full time. Only a handful of crappy doctors take our pathetic excuse for a health insurance company.

"Are you sure you're okay? We're cool, right?" he asks yet again. I nod again. What I want to tell him is that Mama hasn't been to work for the past four weeks and that I worry about whether or not I will have enough money to pay rent and other bills; that I may not even be able to go back to school next term if Mama gets worse and I have to work full time to support the both of us; that I don't even know what I will do if she ... dies. I know people don't die from emphysema over night, but it could happen and she's been getting so much worse with breathing.

The Allens have always been there for us but this time I don't want to rely on them. This time I don't want to rely on anyone. There was a time when Mama and I used to tell the Allens everything, but, for some reason, Mama and I have stopped. Maybe we don't want them to think we need their help, every time we have a crisis. Maybe I want them to know that we finally "made it." I think I want to see if I can do it on my own. The possibility of always having to rely on others to get through life has always made me very uneasy. I shouldn't have to rely on others.

"I wish it would stop snowing. It's spring almost," I finally say, as I notice that crystal flakes have begun to topple onto the cars parked outside.

"We're supposed to get another major snow storm this weekend, too," Davis says.

"Don't remind me," I sign, watching as flakes dust Davis' very old bumblebee yellow Cooper. I think of how Erick drives a brand new one. I think of how easy his life must be. I think of all the scars his privileges have protected him from.

"That's New England for you! Hey, do you wanna go sledding with the kids and me at Lamont Hill on Saturday afternoon? We're going to do a snow dance to the gods tomorrow to ensure optimal blizzard weather." Shaking my head, I sign, "I'd like to but I'm working from six in the morning until nine at night. You don't need to be begging for more snow, dumb ass. What's wrong with you?" I ask, somewhat joking, somewhat annoyed, and completely tired.

"You never work on Saturday. What's up? Do you need money?" I feel my right eye twitch slightly, like it always does, when I begin to stress out about money and on whether or not I should let Davis know. I rub my twitching eye with the back of my right index finger, let out a long controlled breathe, and then reply, "Yea, but I can work for it. I want to work more. I never do anything on Saturday, anyway," I lie. *It's not like it's the only day I can relax. It's not like I'll ever have a free day again, this year—this lifetime.*

He pauses for a moment then picks up his knife and, before he spreads cream cheese on his bagel, looks at me, gesturing if I'd like some before he makes it inedible for my lactose intolerant belly.

"It's all yours. I'm fine, thank you," I say with a long sigh.

"Don't you have a paper due Monday? How are you going to write it on time?" Looking up, he waits for my response.

"Sunday," I sign back.

"Have you done the readings? I thought you were behind on the readings for that class."

"I'm not. I finally did most of the readings," I lie, not even wanting to think about how I will catch up on two weeks worth of reading assignments by this weekend.

"Wow, I'm impressed," he says, his tone indicating that he knows I am lying. He chooses not to confront my lie and changes the subject.

"So, what's Mama Sales up to, lately? Does she still want me to marry you?" I smile then roll my eyes.

"Of course," I sign. Davis grins. We have always had a platonic relationship, even though Davis has made it clear that he wants something more. Men seem to always want more.

"Mama's the same old same old," I kind of mumble.

"You're mumbling."

"She's fine," I sign.

"Olivia said she hasn't seen her in a while. She change offices?" Olivia is Davis' younger sister. She attends elementary school and usually visits Mama in the office, several times a week.

"I think she is working in the back, now," I lie. *Duh! Back of what, Savannah? That's a stupid lie ... Ugh, how am I going to pay this month's heating bill? Maybe it won't be so cold anymore. Should I ask the Allens for help again? No, I can't always rely on them ...*

"Oh?" His tone is obvious and I translate it into, "Feel free to update me on the real story whenever you feel like it, you horrible liar." I want to tell him to stop pressing.

"God, I'm tired," I say with a yawn. I dread getting up at five.

"Have you lost weight? You seem thinner than last month," Davis says.

"A little bit. I haven't been eating much lately. I'm not ..." pausing, I try to remember what 'anorexic' is in sign, but I can't, so I spell it out, "... A-N-O-R-E-X-I-C. You know how my stomach gets when I'm stressed. I can't eat that much."

"I forgot, anorexia is only something, rich, white women with too much time on their hands put themselves through."

"I have never said that."

"You've implied it. You know it's not true, especially since you know it took Elizabeth a long time to come to terms with it and heal." Elizabeth is his twenty-one year old sister. She's been struggling with severe bipolar depression and eating disorders since the age of twelve. While my first day of junior high was greeted with the n-word, hers was met with 'fat-ass Orca the Whale' by some cruel eighth grade girls. At least, that is the story she has told me.

"Sorry," I sign with a half-tired, apologetic smile.

"You know as soon as you start losing a lot of weight, the boobies are the first things to go. That would be quite a loss." He giggles then mouths, "I'm joking." He sighs then mumbles, "God I'm so horny." I pull my hand away from him. Rolling his eyes, he calls me a prude.

"I'm not a freaking prude!" I mouth back to him.

"I'm joking, Savannah! God, a mouth like a sailor these days!" he exclaims, waving his hands in the air, a tentative smile on his warm face. He reaches for my hand and I surprise myself by hiding them on top of my lap, underneath the wooden table. I know Davis is not that jerk from the store, earlier today, but I begin to think of horrible things that I know I shouldn't be. *What if Davis thinks of me that way too? What if he only stays because of something as stupid as my big boobs?*

"That is not true," I whisper to myself, ashamed of even equating Davis with that troll from the store. Lifting my right hand up, I smile to Davis and give him my hand, "Sorry." He nods with a boyish smile, squeezes my hand gently, says, "Okay, let's go, my Nubian princess," then raises the back of my hand to his lips and kisses it gently. Like he always does, he mouths, "Mmmmm … Chocolate!"

No, Davis is not that beast.

CHAPTER FIVE

"How was school, Ms. Savannah Penelope Sales?" Mama asks me. "I never did understand the texture of this crap," I want to say, poking at the slimy okra a la phlegm that has been oozing on my plate for the past ten minutes. The kitchen faucet is leaking on top one of Mama's pans. I wonder if I will ever figure out how to make the leak stop, permanently. It usually starts leaking again, several weeks after I have attempted to fix it. Davis has given it several tries as well. The landlords said that they would have it fixed a month ago. Of course they haven't.

"Fine. I got my paper back from my history class. Jerk gave me a B minus. Thought I was being too subjective ...I can rewrite it though. Don't know why we're reading Jane Austen in a history class."

"You did write the paper the night before, so you shouldn't be too surprised."

"Whatever."

"'Whatever,' nothing."

I carry on with my rant, "He says I simply lack maturity in writing because I am a first year student. I will understand the 'importance' of Jane Austen as I get older. I wanted to tell him that I don't care about white aristocrats and their contrived corny romance problems. It doesn't mean I have a lack of maturity in writing."

"Savannah, you started the damn thing the night before it was due. I'm sorry you didn't get the grade you wanted but you started it the night before it was due. The truth is that you didn't give yourself enough time. In this case you know it ain't got nothing to do with whites. Eventually you're going to have to stop that, you know? We both know it's B.S. but we don't have the power and until we do, you need to stop being so loud about it because you know those teachers aren't ready for it. Anyway, not all white people are out to get you. Anyway, you need to keep your damn grades up, or they'll take away what little financial aid they threw at us. You know they don't care about why you can't do well in school, so just do what the hell you need to do to pass the damn class." My teeth penetrate my lower lip as I try to maintain composure. I mustn't make her upset. I mustn't make her upset. It makes her cough and then she can't breathe when I make her upset.

I lift up the okra slime with my fork then sniff it and wonder how old it is.

"It's only going to get older. If you don't eat it you'll be seeing it on your plate tomorrow … And you know you need to eat it so you don't get constipated. You know you can be a mean little biddy when you don't poop."

"Mama, I'm going to eat it. What else am I going to eat?"

"There was a time when we had nothing to eat, Savannah. Not a goddamn thing."

Yep, heard the story two hundred ninety-nine times, but you can tell me again for the three-hundredth time.

"Well, tomorrow I am making chicken stew. Your future mother-in-law called and said she would drop off some chicken tomorrow morning and some vegetables from their greenhouse, too." This is Davis' mother, Ginger, who Mama jokingly refers to as my 'future mother-in-law.' I wonder if Mama has told Ginger of the "unwanted house guest." She and I had an understanding that we weren't going to tell anyone, just yet.

"It's nice that Ginger gives us the scraps from their highly successful farming business—"

"I never raised you to be so goddamn miserable! Has it really been that bad? It's like you enjoy being miserable." Shrugging, I shove the slimy greens into my mouth. I am the only person I know that eats these phlegmy morsels of rural Southern delight. Mama and Ginger go to Costco, once a month. Mama buys frozen okra in bulk. Lucky me.

Drip, drip … drip … drip, drip …

That freaking piece of crap faucet!

"Sorry. No, it hasn't," I finally answer in a whisper.

"It wasn't easy, Savannah. It still isn't easy, but I tried to give you what I could. We've got a home and we've got food."

There is an awkward silence for several minutes. Then, Mama breaks the silence and says, "Why don't you invite Davis over for dinner? He hasn't been over for dinner since February. Only kid around here I know who likes my okra and my cooking."

"I like your cooking, Mama."

Drip, drip … drip … drip …

"I don't know if he's free tomorrow night. I'll ask him." *Goddamn faucet. Why am I always fixing it? No matter what I do, nothing changes. Nothing changes.*

I put a spoon full of black-eyed peas in my mouth and wash it down with a gulp of Coca-Cola. The sugary carbonation hits an unfilled cavity in the back of my mouth. I huff several times as I let the pain slowly dwindle down.

"Your cavity?" Mama asks me. I simply nod and she replies, "We'll get that taken care of soon, baby." Smiling halfheartedly, I remember that she had made that promise three months ago, just before the emphysema decided to rear its ugly and uninvited head.

"I'll live. It's in a tooth I really don't use too much of. That's why I have so many others. Davis says you only need half your teeth to eat."

"Stop being dumb."

I look down at my plate and I think of how easy Erick's life must be. He and his pretty straight white fucking teeth …

***

April 27, 2005
11:30pm

Dear Diary,

Mrs. Ana Lucia Perez, Esperanza, and I went to The Harvest, the natural grocery that her mother drives to in Glastonbury, Connecticut, twice a month. I am not really into that natural stuff, but Esperanza and Mrs. Perez invited me to come along and then go roller-skating in Hartford, after.

I met a Black guy by the name of Kendell. I was in the bulk herbs aisle, sniffing something called coriander, when I saw him standing at the beginning of the aisle. He hesitated for a moment then made the decision to approach me. I admit, I had thought, "Great, he's going to ask me for money." Kendell did have the goal to ask me for money, but not for what I had assumed it would be for.

When I first looked at him, I could tell he was probably retarded. He just had that type of face that the mentally retarded kids have who are in Special Ed in the west wing of our high school. It was difficult for him to use the left side of his body and I was astonished and humbled about how much effort and tenacity he put into moving his body. His right leg seemed stronger and more coordinated than his left leg. With each step he took, it seemed like he was going to fall over to the left side. I kind of wanted to run away from him, but I know that I shouldn't. I stood there smiling stupidly through gritted teeth as he approached. I remember I had nervously looked around, embarrassed that he was coming my way, praying that Esperanza would rescue me. However, she had been nowhere in sight. Now that I write this, I feel deep shame. But I mean, come on, it's embarrassing that the only other Black person in the entire store is probably begging the mostly white customers for money. And I didn't want people thinking that I was with him.

"Hi ... Roo you have ray minute?" That is what he repeated to me about 4 or 5 times, and he wouldn't give up. After the fifth time, I finally realized he was saying, "Hi, do you have a minute?"

As I tried to understand what he was saying, my heart began to beat rather quickly. The only way I knew what he was asking for was by finally looking at a piece of paper he was holding. My panic began to subside as I realized that the paper said he was raising money for his Special Olympics team. I checked my wallet and could find no money on me. I carefully explained that I had no money on me and apologized. He paused for about five seconds and I could feel that he was negotiating with himself, whether or not he should ask someone else or persuade me more with alternative forms of currency. He did the latter and continued, "Roo you have a keckbook?" He was trying to say checkbook.

I gave him a confused response and said, "No, I'm in high school." He spoke again, saying something like, "You look a lot older." I apologized again and then began looking for Esperanza or Mrs. Perez. I spotted Esperanza, several seconds later. She was down the aisle, walking towards Kendell and me. When Esperanza arrived, Kendell explained what the donations were for and proudly told us that he was the captain of his power lifting team.

We looked at his donation sheet and Esperanza signed her name on line 19 of 20 then gave him five dollars. She asked how long he had been asking people for donations and he said since the beginning of March. He also told us he was twenty years old. It had taken him more than one month to get nineteen donors and less than one hundred fifty dollars. Esperanza cheerfully said, "Good luck dude in finding that twentieth signature and donation." He told Esperanza, "Thank you m'am," and then continued down the aisle towards a white lady in her forties.

As soon as he was out of our earshot, Esperanza started talking about how she had the most respect for this guy. She kept on saying how much it sucked being a dark skinned Black man in this country—let alone a Black man with physical and mental disabilities like Kendell. I had never really thought about that when Kendell first came up to me. I was kind of weirded out and embarrassed—but I didn't tell Esperanza that.

After her rant, which lasted a brief minute, she decided to go find her mother and left me to sniff more funky herbs I had never heard of. After about fifteen minutes passed by, I realized I had not seen Mrs. Perez or Esperanza. I called Esperanza's cell phone, using the cell phone Davis had let me borrow for the day. She told me that she had found Kendell again and was talking to him. Several minutes later, Esperanza found me, explaining that she had talked to Kendell again, and she had given him an additional six dollars (her skating money) in Mrs. Perez's name to complete his twenty necessary signatures.

Within several seconds, Esperanza burst into tears, trying to tell me about Kendell's story. How he had attended college— Stonehill—for the first time last semester; how he had gotten a C—in English and a D in math; how he was not able to continue because the school had taken away his financial aid which was contingent upon a 2.0 GPA or higher.

Esperanza was extremely upset, angry and confused. She kept on asking me why such unfairness was allowed to happen in the USA. "You can just feel that he is such a good person," she said, crying through those words. She continued to tell me that Kendell was now one thousand dollars in debt from school expenses and was expected to pay this off on his own if he wanted to continue towards his Associates degree in physical education. The worse part of the story was that his father had been shot and killed by the Hartford police, "by accident," a few months ago. Therefore he could no longer rely on his father—his guardian—to help him with his debts. "What kind of society punishes Kendell for getting a C—and D when they know what he's dealing with? He has no father. He has no one. Why doesn't anyone care?" After all, her father had been shot and killed in Guatemala, after being falsely labeled as a guerrilla. I kind of got where she was coming from.

But, I stood there, speechless, as she couldn't stop crying. I didn't know what to do.

We didn't go skating.

***

"… Are you sure this price is right? It seems rather expensive," the old lady asks me again. Even though it's cold outside, she is only wearing a brightly multicolored moo moo and what appear to be green house slippers on her feet. It is only two hours into my new Saturday shift and I am about to kill the next whiny customer that approaches me. Currently, I am trying to convince this woman that buying cold medicine from a convenience store is not going to be as cheap as Walmart. She is arguing that at Walmart in Windham, the medicine is nearly half the price of Quikstop's.

"It is the correct price. Quikstop jacks up their prices." I shouldn't be admitting this, but, whatever.

"Walmart doesn't raise their prices." *Lady, does this look like Walmart to you?* She returns my answer with the start of a mucus-filled hacking cough. Her nose is beginning to run. Instead of using a napkin from the counter, she uses the back of her hand.

"Well, I'm never buying medicine from here ever again. This isn't right." She finally hands me her money, then starts coughing again. It sounds as if she is dying this time. Mama comes to mind again and this time, I try to care and ask, "Are you okay?" With watery eyes, she nods, grabs her medicine, and then slowly walks off. I reach into my box of pre-moistened sanitizing hand wipes, strategically placed on the counter by yours truly, and start the disinfecting process. I have too many damn problems and don't need whatever infection the old woman is carrying. If Mama got bronchitis, who knows what would happen?

The store is now empty. I wonder who the next loser will be to bless me with their pointless existence. The morning rush is over and I sigh in relief. Bending over, I grab my backpack and take out a text for Professor Collin's History of South Africa class.

Somehow between the end of the morning rush and my reading assignment, something magical happens. I attribute the catalyst to the moment I decide to pop in my CD of Sade's Lover's Rock. I hit play, sit back down onto my butt-numbing stool, and then turn to the first page of Pumla Gobodo-Madikizela's *A Human Being Died that Night: A South African Woman Confronts the Legacy of Apartheid.*

Sade sings in the background. Lyrics from "It's Only Love That Gets You Through" fill the provincial store with a particular soul and spirit that only she can illicit. As I read Pumla's words, I grin to myself as the music brings back a memory from the previous summer. Esperanza, Davis, and I had been laying out on a meadow laden with black-eyed Susies and poppies somewhere on his family's fifty acres of land, smoking pot. Esperanza had been listening to Sade on my portable Hello Kitty CD player Davis had given to me as an eighteenth birthday present. Her head had been bobbing left and right as she held a half-smoked joint loosely between her succulent Nigerian-Guatemalan lips. She glistens in the sun like one of Ginger's hot strawberry rhubarb pies laying on the sill of an open window. "Sade makes you want to cry, rejoice, fall in love, break up and damn near kill yourself all at the same time," she had proclaimed; her Guatemalan Spanish accent clings onto every syllable.

For fifteen or so minutes, the store is empty and I'm completely enamored by Pumla's personal journey of reconciliation from the people who have murdered and tortured her Black compatriots. Sade's emotional piece, "Slave Song," weaves itself through the air, helping to capture Pumla's passionate journey. I begin thinking of Esperanza again, and the messed up stories she had shared with me and Davis about her own family's escape from the Dirty War Years of Guatemala, the unfortunate family members who were 'disappeared' by the government, and the murder of her Nigerian social activist father. It is at this exact moment that it happens.

The first thing my body becomes aware of is the dramatic change of chemistry within the store's dry and stagnant atmosphere. It is the first sign that something, teetering on the line of this reality and the surreal, is about to emerge. Hints of sweet jasmine and honeysuckle begin to dance around in the air. At first I think I'm imagining it because my memories of Esperanza have such emotional power over me, it has to be psychosomatic. She is the only girl I know who wears this specific perfume oil. She is the only girl I know who infuses these pure botanical essences into Jojoba oil because she is too much of a purist to ever wear a synthetically created fragrance.

The marriage between Tunisian jasmine and French honeysuckle parallel that of the pomp and circumstance of a royal wedding. My entire mind, body, and soul are in awe of this regal and aromatic ceremony.

As my nose continues to receive the delightful flirtations of this perfume, all is quiet on the Western Front. Within the depths of my embittered war trenches, wildflowers begin to grow and blossom.

"Hola."

This is impossible. It can't be her speaking to me right now. She is living in Toronto with her two older sisters and mother now. I must have fallen asleep, and naturally, she has entered my dreams. Naturally, I miss her so dearly that my mind and my nose are playing horrible tricks on my devastated heart.

I refuse to lift my head up from my book, afraid that if it really is her, my stomach will become the victim of a massive mutant butterfly attack. Until this very moment, it has never occurred to me that my fantasy of her returning to America so soon could possibly be something I'm not emotionally ready for. Perhaps this is why some hidden desires are best kept in the realm of fata morgana.

This is simply not happening. I tell myself, *Keep your head down, eyes on the prose, and ears on Sade.* But how does one release their heart from a voice—the very voice—that had originally captured it? Upon capture, had not caged the thick skinned heart but in fact released it into the world of the unknown, much scarier, yet unquestionably more exhilarating, than that comfortable cage?

I refuse to look up. She responds to my silence by leaning over. With my peripheral vision, I see two golden brown hands lay themselves directly in front my book, one on top of the other. Her head follows, chin lying on top of her hands, mirroring my reading position. As the jasmine and honeysuckle envelop me, the butterflies in my stomach begin to grow. For several seconds—may be longer—she does nothing. Perhaps she thinks I have fallen asleep, much like I used to while reading boring homework assignments in study hall. Finally, a careful whisper flows from her lips, "Savannah Penelope Sales, have you fallen asleep on the job?"

She waits for me to say or do something. What do I say? What do I do?

I decide to play along and pretend that I in fact have dozed off while at work. *When I wake up to her, how shall I respond? Do I act surprised? Do I fall off my chair followed by tears of joy? Do I 'scream like a girl?' Eight months. It's been eight months!*

I decide that I will jump out of my chair, look confused for several seconds then, upon realization that Esperanza is here and not at the University of Toronto where she thinks I think she is, I will "scream like a girl." I temporarily forget that I'm 5'1" and not sitting on a regular chair but on a high stool in which my short legs dangle quite a bit; Davis, who is nearly 6'4," says that in it I look like a "baby in a high chair." Hence, naturally, when I jump up out of my 'supposed sleep,' I forget there is no bottom beneath my short legs. I loose my balance, careening into the blue speckled dirty ivory linoleum floor. Make no mistake, I scream 'like a girl' for real.

Esperanza completely loses it. It never takes much to make her burst out into uncontrollable laughter. Before I know it, she's in back of the counter, still cackling, helping me to my feet, exclaiming, "Lo siento, pobrecita. Are you okay?" And there she is, standing mere inches away from me; this six foot beauty with the physique of an Olympic tri-athlete and spirit as clean and pure as artesian spring water, all meticulously wrapped up with the transparent confidence of a seasoned Haute Couture model.

"Surprise! I'm back!" she announces. I force the butterflies in my stomach to crash into a brick wall. I try to compose myself but I can feel my body trembling, eyes resisting the temptation to respond to her presence with a geyser of tears.

"What, no hu—" before she can finish, I am embracing her as if I have rediscovered a long lost teddy bear from my early childhood. I almost don't want to let go because I'm still not sure if this is real or not. She let's me hold her in my embrace as long as I need. I am not sure how many seconds go by before I decide to finally let her go.

"You're supposed to be in Toronto," I say in a tentative whisper. Her strong brown hands grab mine. With a mischievous grimace, she leans over to my ear, "Happy Birthday. I wanted to surprise you. What better present than me? I told Davis to keep it a secret. We planned this months ago!" She pulls away from my ear, bites her cute lower lip, and then patiently waits for my response. I am speechless.

"You and he d-d-did this ... for me?" I stutter.

"Of course we did. We love you!" she says with a giggle. She squeezes my hands tighter, "Here's the deal: You know how I decided not to enroll into classes this term and instead accept that amazing research assistant internship at the TPOR—Toronto Organization for Political Refugees?" I nod slowly and she continues, "Well, they were so impressed with my brilliance, grant proposal writing abilities, and awareness of 'the issues'—" She let's go of my hands, raises her arms up and does 'air quotes' with her fingers, "—that they are sending me to a two month long symposium of workshops, classes, kick ass speakers and what not, all taking place at University of Connecticut. I wrote up a grant proposal to get funding from this foundation just outside of Toronto. We got this huge grant from the founder, this rich philanthropist lady who—Get this!—happens to support female activists from the global South, that want to continue their activism while attending a Canadian university. Apparently she's the daughter of some dead guy who used to be uber rich, oppressive, and imperialistic and made his fortune off the blood, sweat and tears of brown backs in Mexico and investments during South African apartheid. TPOR asked me to pick an institute to go to—anywhere in Canada or USA—to support our work. I rummaged through—Am I using that word right?—the million pamphlets and brochures we received about human rights stuff, hoping to find something in Connecticut and as close to East Lebanon as possible, and suddenly it appeared in my hands!: A brochure about UConn hosting the 2007 International Human Rights Symposium for Student Activists … Am I clever or what?" She ends by putting her hands on her hips and cocking her head to the left side. She is very clever and anyone who talks to her for the first time will realize within a minute why she graduated salutatorian with a full scholarship waiting for her at University of Toronto.

"You did this for me?" I repeat. She nods with raised eyebrows, then looks me up and down and asks, "Chica, did you lose weight?" She takes her left index finger and pokes it inside of the waistband to my orange corduroy pants I had made senior year in high school. The warmth of her finger grazes my pierced belly button. We had both gotten our belly buttons pierced during her eighteenth birthday, last May. I inspired her, after having my nose and eyebrow pierced for my eighteenth birthday. A month after her birthday, she had decided to pierce her tongue and ended up speaking with a lisp for nearly two months. Her touch creates a billion more mutant butterflies in my stomach.

"OK sweetie, the good news is that I'm here! The bad news is that I have orientation in forty-five minutes. My flight got in at eleven last night. I wanted to see you then but I didn't think you'd appreciate me ringing your doorbell so late. So, here I am because I just couldn't wait to see my favorite girl. So I got up this morning to drive from Mansfield to see you, where I'm staying with this awesome professor and her husband for two months. But now I have to head back for orientation. I could have gotten up earlier to spend more time here but I was exhausted and literally slept through my alarm clock so please don't kill me when I tell you I have to leave in a few minutes to race to Storrs." She speaks enthusiastically and at one million miles per hour. She has always been full of energy and extremely hyper, the complete antithesis of myself.

"You have to go?" *That's all you have to say, Savannah? Say something. Tell her you're happy to see her ...You are happy to see her, right? Say something you idiot!*

"Yes, but I'll be back. I just had to come and see you; I didn't care if it was even for a few minutes. So listen, I have to go—" she interrupts herself and gives me another hug and kiss on the cheek, "God, it is so good to finally be here, with you!" I smile, nod, and then finally give myself a mental slap in the face to wake up out of my stupidity and anxiety induced mind freeze, "I really missed you, Esperanza."

"Of course you did. We're going to have a blast!—Hey, they finally got Fair Trade coffee here! Not that it makes up for selling evil Coca-Cola. You aren't drinking Coke still, are you?"

"Kitter saw the advertisement for Newman's Organic coffee, at McDonalds, and decided to sell Fair Trade and Organic. Customers like it a lot and didn't complain too much about the price increase ... I didn't know about Coke. What's wrong with Coke?"

"I sent you a newsletter to your email account last week. Hello! Mad human rights violations on my peoples in South and Central America! India too!"

"Sorry, I haven't read it yet. It's kind of hard to boycott everything, you know?" I think about how last week, in the library, I downloaded an application from Coca-Cola's Two Year Colleges scholarship web page. *How evil can they really be?*

"Yea, but it's not like you need to drink Coke to survive. Anyway I have to go now," she says, looking at her digital sports watch, "because orientation is, like, mandatory and I don't want to support the whole CP time stereotype for our people."

"You're insane," I say, simultaneously wondering if I should read the newsletter she sent me, or if I should delete it so I can apply for the scholarship without worrying how Coca-Cola makes its profits.

"Takes one to know one!" She leans over, hugs me again, "I'm calling you as soon as I get home from the workshops, okay?"

"You're back," I whisper, not wanting to let go again.

"But I gotta go! Let a sistah go, okay?" She says, gently pulling out of our hug. She blows me a kiss then bolts out of the store. I hurry to the window to see her as she jumps into an old blue Volkswagen Rabbit. I giggle as she nearly rolls back into another car, entering the lot. Girl could never figure out stick shift. I see her mouth, "Dammit!" and then hear her try to shift and grind the gears into first. Eventually, she zooms out of the parking lot without stopping at the intersection. An old pickup truck, hauling bales of hay, nearly hits her. I could never figure out how she passed her driver's test while I failed mine twice.

I can still hear my heart beating furiously. I stand there, frozen for several minutes, in shock, until unresolved feelings begin to thaw out. It had been the physical distance between us that had helped me suppress these feelings.

I startle myself with a choking sound in my throat. "Don't cry. You can control it," I whisper to myself. I clench my fists and repeat, "You can control it."

***

It isn't something I try to think about. Since Esperanza left eight months ago, I have blocked it out of my head. This isn't too difficult when I am worrying about Mama, trying to make enough money, and struggling to stay in school. I had totally convinced myself that I really wasn't like that; that I would simply forget about it and keep it buried in the back of my mind. Seeing her—smelling her—had made it all come back in a flash.

Sighing, I turn over on my side and look at my clock. It is a little past three in the morning. Having gone to bed nearly two hours ago, and rather physically exhausted, I have yet to fallen asleep. I am consumed with my own denial; an identity I have prayed I will never be forced to come to terms with; an identity I have convinced myself I can virtually make disappear by simply focusing on other stressful aspects of this chaos called my life.

Go to sleep, Savannah. You have to get up by six to start working on this stupid paper. Closing my eyes, I try to clear my tangled mind to go to sleep. However, the image of her enters my mind. Soon, I recollect the first time I realized, without a doubt, that I felt it with her. I had never felt that way about anyone else before …

¿... Quieres algunas flores?" Esperanza asks me. We are both sitting up against the big oak tree in the back of her family's yard. It is August 2003 and I am wearing orange cotton drawstring Capri pants. She is wearing a white skirt without a slip, revealing the silhouette of white bikini underwear. Both of us are wearing identical purple halter-tops we had bought at the mall, earlier that week. Esperanza hands me several Echinacea flowers she has extracted from her mother's medicinal garden. She isn't supposed to do that, but Esperanza has always been a rebel.

"Gracias," I reply, accepting the flowers and continuing, "I can't believe school starts in two weeks. We've got so much to do, still!" I then try to put one of the flowers in my hair. I am wearing two afro puffs and wonder how the flowers will fit.

"Let me help you. I love when you wear your hair like this. You should sport the afro puffs all the time. I'm glad your electric hot comb broke. You don't need to be straightening this bounty of curly haired glory." She takes the flower and sticks it into one of my chestnut colored afro puffs. As she giggles sweetly, I suddenly feel an emotion I have never felt before: love's rapture.

She takes another flower and sticks it into the other puff. "You look so unbelievably cute. Why do you straighten it all the time with that silly hot comb? You weren't doing that when I first met you."

"I have to," I say. I look down at the ground and tell myself not to think about how great she smells ... and how much I would like her to touch me again.

"It's going to be hot as hell today, again. Should we chill in the Allen's pond again?" she suggests. I don't know how I will handle seeing her in her baby blue bikini again, those long perfect golden brown legs, kicking in the water.

"That sounds good." She puts her arm around me, "Stop bumming. We've got two weeks. If you were a day fly that would be fourteen lifetimes and how cool is that?" She kisses me on the cheek like she always does, but this time my body reacts to it in a way I have never experienced. At first, I think the wetness in my GAP panties is my period suddenly starting a week early. However, a

euphoric tingling follows the wetness and I realize that this isn't my period.

"Oh crap!" I exclaim.

"What?"

"Uh-um—I think I started my period." I jump up and run straight towards her house. I hear her yelling in the background, "Tampons are in the second drawer!"

Before I know it, I'm in the second floor olive-green decorated bathroom that Esperanza shares with two younger sisters. I am sitting on the floor, back pressed up against the locked door, Capri pants and panties around my ankles, my brown fingers oscillating inside that tender wetness, wishing that it were her that is inside of me ...

***

"I got her newsletter about Coca-Cola last week, but deleted it. I wasn't really interested," Davis tells me as he pulls into Stonehill Community College's parking lot B. It is Monday afternoon and my Quikstop shift has just ended. Davis teaches Sign to children across campus at the Human and Child Development Center.

"Well, good to see that Toronto hasn't changed her or her activism, you know?" I sign, after he parks the Cooper into a space between a dilapidated and faded brown Dustan sedan and an old silver Vespa moped.

"I guess. I just hope she doesn't turn into an anarchist or whatever. She's too cute and smart for that. Does she always have to send us those newsletters about how everything is evil? Remember she didn't talk to you for a week, last March, because you didn't want to go protest the war in Iraq at the East Lebanon town hall?"

"What do you mean you don't want to come? You told me 'yes,' last night," Esperanza tells me.

"We're going to be the only brown and Black people in a crowd of white teenagers. When the mayor calls the cops, who do you think will get beaten and hauled off to jail, first?"

"Well, it's worth the risk. I'd trade being beaten and thrown in jail in a heartbeat if it frees thousands of suffering Iraqis. Did you

not get the e-newsletter I sent to you about the females who have been raped by the US soldiers?"

"Well, I didn't put them in that situation and I can't help it if cops scare me."

"Where do you think your federally taxed dollars go, every time you get your paycheck from Quikstop? Shit, you can be such an American sometimes!"

"Why are my best friends an anarchist and an angry Black militant nationalist?" Davis asks, shaking his head.

"Shut up," I sign back. He giggles in response then continues, "Anyway, when are we going to eat some more of mama's fried chicken? I used to get invites all the time. What's up?"

"I left a message on your voicemail, Friday," I sign back.

"Well, I didn't get it unless Olivia erased the message without telling me who called. She's always doing that stupid crap." I yawn for the tenth time. I feel as if I am going to fall asleep right here and now.

"You look like crap," he tells me, turning the engine off. You would too if you didn't go to sleep because you were writing the most pathetic excuse for academic scholarship.

"Long night," I sign.

"Your paper?" I nod, "If he gives me a C, I will be happy."

"Ouch ... that bad?"

"Yes. I may drop the class."

"Maybe you should cut back on your Saturday hours after all."

"That's okay—There he is," I suddenly interrupt myself because Erick Roberts has parked about fifty feet away from us, in his brand new red Mini Cooper with an annoying Thule ski rack on top of it and two *PETA* stickers stuck on the rear bumper.

"Who?" Davis signs.

"Erick Roberts. My arch nemesis!" I end up spelling everything out since I don't know the word 'arch nemesis' in Sign. We both watch as Erick gets out of his car. As usual, Erick is clean and pristine; complete with another fashionable outfit I have never seen him wear before.

"Wow, he really is preppie ... Still, you shouldn't be so bitter towards him." I sigh and call Davis an idiot as his head turns away from me.

***

I catch myself falling asleep again for the fifth time and jerk my head to wake myself up. It is only fifteen minutes into my Sociology class. I wonder how I will be able to stay awake for the next fifty minutes. Rogards is talking and I try to focus back onto what he is saying. Something about welfare and its history in the nineteenth century. Rogards has a very monotone voice, perfect to fall asleep to. I look at my watch and blink my eyes hard. I should have had more than one cup of coffee ... I'm so hungry.

Laying the side of my head on my hand, I listen to Rogards and try to take notes. Before I know it, I am drifting...

—"Savannah!" I nearly jump out of my seat. For about two-seconds, I forget I am sitting in class. Professor Rogards is standing right next to me. I quickly turn my head left to right and realize my classmates are looking at me. Shit, I fell asleep.

"You're snoring. I was under the impression that my class got you all fired up." I wonder what time it is. How long had I been asleep? Damn it.

"Sorry." They're all looking at me. *Laughing at me quietly, 'Finally, the bitter Black bitch screwed up.' That's what they are thinking ... Erick must be loving this.*

"Long weekend?" Rogards asks me. I nod. What else can I do? I try not to think about how embarrassed I am feeling. It isn't fair.

"That's good ... Did you happen to catch the readings for today?" I nod, still not quite awake—Oops, I should have shaken my head. The assignment is still on my To Do list, as I'm only halfway through the book. *Now he is going to ask me a question about it. Don't tell him you didn't read the whole thing, dumb ass.*

"His approach to welfare nicely parallels your argument from last week."

I am about to open my mouth to try to respond when Rogards interrupts, "Actually, can you save it for Wednesday? I didn't realize that class is almost over. We've got about a minute left and you usually end up starting an hour long debate with your peers." Grinning at me, I realize that maybe he still views me as a somewhat responsible student.

Everyone shuffles their belongings together. Shoving my notebook into my backpack, I stand up quickly and put my coat on.

"Savannah?" Shoot, it is Erick's voice. I sigh, wondering if I should even turn around to see what he wants.

"I know you hear me." I turn around, "Yea?" He is still sitting at his desk. So, he's going to stay an extra few minutes just to irritate me? He removes his *Oliver Peoples* red plastic framed reading glasses from his chiseled face. He has a slight sunburn on his nose, probably from having gone skiing up in New Hampshire like he always does.

"I have another class to get to, Erick."

"It'll only take a second ... The other day, you said some ... things." Great, he's still 'traumatized' over last week. Now, he's going to throw it in my face how much of a loser I am for falling asleep. I don't need this shit.

I grab my book, *A Human Being Died That Night*, for my next class. How the hell does Pumla forgive any of these people?

"Well?" I ask him.

"Well, I thought about it and I think I may ... well, need to—well—reevaluate my identity and what it really means to be ... well, me." Someone pinch me! Am I dreaming? Did I fall asleep in class again? I did not just convince a privileged white boy that he needs to think!

"Are you kidding me?" I ask him, looking down at Pumla's book, wondering, What would Pumla do? I know Erick is nothing compared to that white nationalist guy she interviewed for months, but ...

"No, I'm not. What you said last class, like, really pissed me off and it's been nagging at me for, like, ever." I cringe as he uses 'like.' He uses it too often and it drives me crazy how superficial it makes him sound.

"Savannah, I'm not a racist. I know this. But then you, last week ..."

"I 'what' last week?"

"You've decided otherwise and I just can't let it go." I sigh and roll my eyes, "So, what do you want me to do about it?" He rubs his palm over his throat. I notice a scar on the left side of his neck that I had never noticed before. Maybe it's because he usually wears those annoying turtleneck Lacoste shirts and sweaters.

"I honest to God don't mean to offend anyone, but I guess I do, and I don't like it. I don't want people of color—don't be offended by that—"

"I'm not." *Wow, this is so cliché. Did he rehearse this from a script?*

"I don't want people of color always hating me for something I clearly can't see that I'm doing wrong, per se. Especially if you say that white male privilege protects me from everything evil in the world," he says, massaging the scar on his neck again. His tone is half nervous, half annoyed ... but sincere.

"So, you want me to give you a reading list of the top ten books by Black and brown folk to cure you of this? Let's start off with Toni Morrison's *The Bluest Eye* and Damali Ayo's *How to Rent a Negro* and you can write up a book report for me for next class." He raises his eyebrows in slight confusion, trying to read my tone of voice as serious or sarcastic. After several seconds, he realizes I am nowhere near the land of serious.

"Savannah, take me seriously. And yes, I know who Toni Morrison is. I saw the movie Beloved." He looks at me intensely, takes a breath, and then continues, "Can you take an hour or two out of your schedule to perhaps sit down with me to tell me what I do that offends or may offend people of color? Tell me about the oblivious white privilege you are constantly accusing me of enacting?"

Gritting my teeth, I do not know how to respond to this. My brain is behaving incoherently from exhaustion. It's not like I can speak for all people of color, either. Is he asking me to enlighten him within a mere two hours? How can he possibly ignore his life long years of unadulterated and uncontested practice of nauseating entitlement? What am I, the Magic White-Guilt-Free fairy? He will not understand it. He would not understand it. Being Black has to be lived, breathed, smelled, and tasted. How dare he expect me to show him 'the way' in such a limited time?—And for free no less! I think I'm going to charge the jerk.

He looks up at me, awaiting my reply. I want to punch him in his thin nose and scream loud enough that even my dead overworked and under-appreciated ancestors can hear, "The damage is already done! Nothing I will ever say can make you change it. Nothing! You'll forget what I've said in a matter of hours!"

I look at the annoying Lacoste alligator symbol on his shirt and, for some reason, think of Mama. Pumla's book still in my hands, I'm reminded of something Mama has said, many times. The words unravel from my memory and resonate in the back of my head, as if coming from an antique phonograph from the corner of a dusty attic, "You can lead a horse to water, but sometimes you can't make him drink."

Taking one last look at the book, I put it back in my bag.

So, is he the horse or am I?

***

"Esperanza and I had lunch today," Davis tells me as I take a bite out of my Macintosh apple. Macintosh apples are the few things I like about living in East Lebanon because farmers like to grow them everywhere and they happen to be my favorite apple. We are sitting in Violet's Café at our usual table at the usual evening time.

"We drove around forever to find a restaurant that serves vegan food and fair-trade teas and coffee," he says.

"Why the hell is she a vegan now?" I roll my eyes, remembering how, two years ago, she had decided to turn into a vegetarian and it drove her mama crazy. She had been given a *PETA* pamphlet by some crazy white protestor at a *KFC* in Willimantic. She and I had been walking by it to get to the fabric store. This short and fat white lady was screaming, "Animals are the new slaves!" I told Esperanza not to take the pamphlet, but she did anyway. For two weeks straight, she would not stop telling me how cows are enslaved "just like Black people were." There was even one point in which she threatened to end our friendship if I didn't stop eating Chicken McNuggets. I literally told her, "*Kiss my Black ass.*" She didn't talk to me for two weeks.

"It's her new thing. I mean, I get that her dad was murdered because of coffee and cocoa, but now she wants to stop drinking milk and eating eggs because she says it's all the same thing. I told her that she didn't know what she was talking about and that all our cows are treated really well and humanely."

"Oh lord, I'm not interested in going through this crap with her again."

"I don't know, maybe it won't be as bad as it was last time. We found a place called VegPlanet and all I was allowed to eat was a fermented tofu burger called tiki, or temple, or something weird on gluten-free bread. I don't get it. Whatever, I guess it's her new thing—"

"Her 'new thing?'"

"Yea, some new natural diet based on compassionate consumption. We had some nasty brownie—" he air quotes the 'brownie,' "made from rice milk and carob and some other nasty crap. Her face looks really cleared up from acne, though, and she claims it's the 'vegan way,'" he emphasizes his pronunciation of 'vegan way' as if it is some esoteric mysterious path to enlightenment. I giggle.

"I remember when Mama tried to convince me that carob was just as good as chocolate," I say, shaking my head as I try to get the memory of that blasphemous taste out of my mind. When she realized that I was lactose intolerant and some lady at school found out, she gave Mama some carob and soy powder and promised her that I wouldn't be able to tell the difference between that and chocolate milk. Did it work? Hell no. She ended up mixing Hershey's cocoa and Domino sugar to get me to drink soymilk during my childhood. She thought it was cheaper to make it from powder then to buy packaged soy chocolate milk all the time.

Realizing that Davis hadn't asked me to come along for lunch, I whine, "Hello, you could have invited me!"

"Maybe we're planning a birthday surprise for you," he says with his signature boyish grin. I shrug and look at my watch, trying not to show my grin of appreciation. *Wow, I'm going to be nineteen this month. How'd that happen so fast?*

"Am I boring you?" he asks. Shaking my head, "Of course not. I am trying to stay awake." It is a little after four-thirty and I don't even know how I will handle working from seven-thirty until midnight tonight.

"So, like I was saying, other than talking about your birthday—"

"I hate surprises."

"Everyone pretends to hate them and they love them." I shrug again. He continues, "We were talking about getting together soon to go bowling. She said she would call you tonight to arrange something."

"But I'm working 'til forever tonight." I shake my head and then pout my lips.

"Well, whose fault is that? If you need to borrow money from us …"

"Whatever, we're fine. If I need more money, I work for it." Davis begins scratching some dried food off of the cherry wood table with the nail to his right index finger.

"Savi, what is up with you day today? You're kind of bitchy."

"I'm always bitchy—and do you have to do that? It's kind of gross." He stops scratching the table and says, "Well, you're bitchier than normal."

"I did something stupid," I begin. His eyes light up with curiosity, "Which was …?"

"I told that jerk that I'd tell him why he's an offensive elitist." I roll my eyes and start shaking my head in disbelief from my interactions with Erick.

"That jerk?"

"Erick Roberts."

"Whoa … Back up and tell me what you're babbling about." I hesitate for a second and realize that maybe I shouldn't have brought it up. However, it's just bugging the hell out of me that, for some stupid reason, I told Erick I would do what he had requested. *Isa be a nurturing shuffling mammy for the dumb white boy when all he needs is a good bitch slap.*

Five minutes later, I have finished telling Davis what happened between Erick and I.

"That was stupid," Davis agrees. Before I can chime in with another sentence, he continues, "Unless someone has had a crush on him all along but could only express it through verbally aggressive behavior because she could never live with herself for being in love with a rich white boy. Anyway, I'm way hotter than him—"

"Shut up," I sign.

"Whatever." I look at him, annoyed, because we both know how he feels about me. As much as the fact he is my best friend, I know the possibility of me being in love with someone else, is something he doesn't want to fathom.

"There is no way I have a crush on him. I could never like a boy—I mean, that boy."

"Denial," he continues. Why even bother arguing? Funny, after sixteen years of friendship, he never suspected that I could be ... well, you know ...

I lay my head down on the table, exacerbated. I am feeling sick to my stomach all of a sudden. My stomach doesn't do well when I'm overly exhausted. For some peculiar reason, the small cafe's daily mélange of coffee, sweet pastries, and traces of cigarette breath are repulsively pungent ...

"Savannah, wake up ... Savi?" I lift my head up slowly, in response to Davis' persistent voice.

"It's seven-twenty."

"No!" I exclaim. Quickly looking outside, I see it is dark ... and snowing again. Yawning, I sign, "Damn it, I'm going to be late ... You watched me sleep all this time? Wasn't that boring?"

"Yea, but you needed it. Caught up on my lesson plans for next week and started reading *The Kite Runner*," he says, closing his notebook and laying his pen on top of the table, "Feeling better?" I nod and lay my head back down on the table.

***

The phone rings as soon as I walk through our front door. It is a little past midnight. Mama is in bed. Before I can pick the phone up, the answering machine turns on, "Hola Savi. I know you're there." I immediately rush to the phone at the sound of Esperanza's voice.

"Hello, I'm here."

"What are you up to? I didn't wake you up, did I?"

"No, I just got home from Hellstop."

"I saw Davis today. We wanted to go bowling or something. I decided to work it around your schedule since you're busier than all of us. You interested?"

"Hell's yeah!" Trying to think of when I can do this, Thursday evening, after eight, comes to mind.

"Thursday after eight—Oh no, I'm meeting with Erick. Damn it!"

"It's okay." No, it's not! Erick, you're about to screw everything up.

"Who's Erick?"

"Some dude."

"Why don't you bring him along?" *So Davis can think I am in love with this guy and make stupid comments? Whatever. Who cares what he thinks? He's so junior high.*

I reluctantly oblige with a less than enthusiastic, "Sure, whatever …So, have you settled into your room?"

"Yea. The professor is mad cool and she and her husband are throwing me a welcome party, soon, even though I'm only going to be here for three months. Of course you and Davis are invited."

"Cool."

"Oh, did Davis tell you about that great vegan restaurant we went to this afternoon? I think you and I should definitely go there soon! They have really good organic tempeh burgers."

"Sounds good," I lie, following it with a long tired yawn.

"Do you know what tempeh is?"

"Of course I do!" I try to reply as enthusiastically as possible as I tap into my brain to remember Davis' description of the food he had eaten with her, "It's fermented soy!"

"So, you've had it before?" She asks.

"Not yet."

"Then we definitely have to do it! And they've got some great brownies too. Maybe I can pick you up for lunch one afternoon next week when the professor is away. She said I can use the car when she's not there."

"I am not getting in a car with you unless it's an automatic. I saw you tear out of Quikstop's parking lot the other day."

"Yo, that's cold, girl! You flunked your test twice and you don't want to get in a car with me?" We both laugh.

"OK chica, I'll let you go to bed. I think I keep hearing you yawn on the other end," she finishes.

"Sorry," I say through another yawn, "Long day."

"No problem. Buenas noches—Oh, and let me know if your date is a vegetarian or vegan so we can all plan where we can all eat after bowling." I am too tired to correct her choice of the word 'date,' or to be annoyed about not being able to eat some good ass chicken on Thursday night.

"I'll let you know. Have a great sleep, girl."

"You too. Ciao!"

CHAPTER SIX

July 2004

"How'd your Mama teach how you how to do this so well? It looks hard. It's so beautiful," Esperanza asks me, as I finish cornrowing the last section of her hair. We are sitting in her backyard. Esperanza is looking into her hand held mirror. It is another warm Saturday. I look over her shoulder and peer into the mirror as well. We both smile and she kisses me on the cheek, "You're so good at this! You should open up a salon in East Lebanon, girl! White folk are into cornrows and braids these days. Remember when Emily and Tina got back from Barbados with their hair in cornrows? They thought they were the shit."

As I lovingly weave each strand of her curly shiny brown hair into perfect rows, I sigh and respond, "Emily asked me why I didn't cornrow my hair since everyone in Barbados does it."

"So, she's met every Black person in Barbados to draw this conclusion?"

"Apparently she's hip to what our people do on the islands."

"Paleaaassse!" We both start giggling as I finish the last braid, "All done, sweetie."

"Thanks!" I sit down beside her. Her mix of Lavender and Jasmine body oil teases my sixteen-year-old nose.

"We're twins!" she says, looking at both of our braided hairstyles in her mirror.

"Two beautiful brown princesas. Fuck Snow White! We're real royalty!" She says, rather loudly. She has started swearing profusely in the past year. It's probably because I have sworn since I can remember, and it's rubbed off on her. Mama never said I couldn't cuss. I remember one evening, after arguing with the tenant about playing her guitar too loud, Mama slammed the door and bellowed, 'God fucking dammit cunt of a whore!' I had been trying to read Langston Hughes' *Black Misery* on the floor of the living room when the slamming of the heavy oak door startled me. (Actually, I was reading a Barbie storybook about the beach and had

63

slipped it underneath the Hughes' book as soon as I had heard the door slam. Mama had picked the book up for five cents at some rummage sale and told me I should try to read that before reading anything else.)

Mama responded to a startled daughter by folding her arms quickly, cocking her head, then, without an ounce of shame, "It's therapy. There's just something so good about saying shit, fuck and everything in between when you've had a day in which everyone pisses you off and cuttin' and shootin' them will just land you on death row." I was six years old.

"You're so gorgeous, Esperanza." I finish the compliment with a hopeless sigh. With my mouth closed, I run my tongue along my crooked teeth.

"What's that all about? You're beautiful, Savannah."

"I know," I lie, feeling the ugly scar on my head with the tips of my fingers.

"Do you?" Beside Mama, Mrs. Perez, Davis, and Esperanza, no one has ever told me this. Mama and Davis don't really count. Mamas are supposed to tell their children that they are beautiful. Anyway, Davis feels like a brother to me.

Closing my eyes and leaning my head on Esperanza, I bitterly recall Tommy Snade, during recess, pointing to dog feces and telling everyone that it was the same color as my skin.

"Savi, if you don't think you're a beautiful human being—"

"I'm trying," I say, smiling in the mirror to reveal the huge gap in between my teeth that has always reminded me of a Black plantation mammy. *All I need is a head rag and pig lard smeared all over my face.* I crunch my nose several times in the mirror, scrutinizing the big flat thing.

"And you better be joking about getting a nose job if you ever won the lottery," she warns.

"It's for practical reasons. My bridge is so flat that my sunglasses are always sliding down!"

"You're crazy."

"I know."

***

"He's coming along?" Davis asks me. It's seven forty-five, Thursday evening at Quikstop. I sip my Coke, "Unfortunately, yes." I did read the newsletter Esperanza sent. Yes, the company is horrible, and they have committed human rights violations throughout the world, including Guatemala, up the wazoo ... But damn, it just taste so good ... and that scholarship would be mad cool if I could get it. I can't boycott everything.

"What?"

"Yes!" Why am I screaming? He can't hear me. I sign it.

"But you hate him," he signs back.

"I don't hate him. He just bothers me during class discussion."

"You're in love." I roll my eyes, "You're so junior high."

"He volunteered to drive us all. It's safer than your ... D-E-A-T-H-T-R-A-P car."

"That deathtrap's hauled your ass everywhere for the past three years, Ms. I-Can't-Pass-My-Driver's-Test ... I can't believe he's coming. Can I ask him why he's attending Stonehill if he's so well-off?"

"You can ask him whatever the hell you want. I just know he told the class his lame reason for enrolling. He felt like taking this class because he says he has a little time before he starts his new job in the summer. Since he'll be the CFO of some nonprofit that helps low-income people living with AIDS and HIV, he thought it would be nice to take a class about po' folk. His organization is actually paying for this class and some other class he's enrolled in to learn how to use some financial software."

"Isn't he a little young to be a CFO?"

"I don't know and I don't care."

"Do you really think you're going to change the way this dude looks at the world?"

"Hell no!" I say.

Several minutes later, Mr. Erick Roberts enters Quikstop. He is wearing perfectly pressed khakis with a tan turtleneck sweater, a little *Lacoste* crocodile on the breast.

"We're going bowling, not playing croquet," I whisper to myself.

CHAPTER 6

"What's up?" I greet Erick.

"Not much."

"Find the place okay?"

"A little confusing to drive at night. Half the roads have signs. Why doesn't this town have streetlights? Pretty dangerous ..."

"To make your life more difficult, because it's all about you, Erick. You." Okay, I don't actually say that. I'm supposed to be nice. Tonight I have transformed into the Magic White-Guilt-Free Fairy. *Hmmmm, now if I could only remember where I left my magic wand and dust.*

"You sure you wanna drive us to the bowling alley?" I ask him, trying to put as much concern into my voice as possible.

"Sure ..." I look at Davis as he waits for me to introduce him. Finally, I do, "Erick, Davison Ryan Allen the third." They both shake hands. I wonder how he will respond to Davis? Earlier, I had told Erick that Davis was deaf. However, a second later, Davis and I are both surprised as Erick replies in Sign, "Nice to meet you." How long did that take you to rehearse, Captain America?

"Savannah didn't tell me you know Sign," Davis signs back. I cannot tell if he is being sarcastic or not. As I look at both of them, I realize just how opposite their styles are. Davis, with his long brown hair in a braided ponytail, jeans, wearing his favorite black tee shirt with icon *The Rock*, a.k.a. Dwanye Johnson, plastered on it. Two surgical steel earplugs pierce each ear lobes. Since Davis wasn't getting his belly button pierced with Esperanza and I, on her birthday last year, we persuaded him to get a piercing to honor our dear friend. Mother Allen was not happy.

"My little sister is hearing impaired," he replies in sign. What are the chances?

"I guess that means we can't talk about you, huh?" Davis jokes, nudging Erick.

"Don't scare him," I sign to Davis.

"Anyway, no one calls me Davison. I just go by Davis. Our friend Esperanza lives close to the bowling alley, so she'll be meeting us there," Davis says. I sit down on the stool behind the counter, anxiously waiting for the last few minutes of my shift to end.

"So, do you live in East Lebanon too?" Erick asks Davis.

"All my life, on a dairy farm."

"I never knew Connecticut had farming towns until I moved here." But you know everything, I think to myself, already becoming irritated with his presence.

"Savi says you went to school in Boston?"

"Cambridge, actually. Did my undergrad at Harvard and got my MBA from Sloan at MIT." *Big whoopee. You wanna doggie biscuit?*

Davis tells Erick how he will be attending University of Wisconsin-Madison this fall and that he had deferred a year to teach kids Sign at Stonehill.

As the clock slowly ticks towards seven, I listen as they bond over food I can't eat or drink. Erick tells us how he spent his vacation in Italy for four weeks, last summer, eating "the finest cheeses" and drinking the "best wines" in Tuscany with his sister, Katherine Privileged-White-Girl-in-Training, who is getting a PhD in wine science at University of California, Davis. Davis excitedly tells him that his focus in college will be on cheese science.

I sigh in annoyance; they're not supposed to like each other. This is going to be a long night.

CHAPTER SEVEN

"Savannah is kicking our asses!" Davis exclaims, as he looks up at the bowling scoreboard. We are in the town of Windham, next door to East Lebanon and home of Stonehill. Esperanza and Davis are competing against Erick and I. We've been here for about twenty minutes and I have yet to give Erick his lesson. I don't even know how the hell to start this crap. What the hell had I been thinking anyway? This is certainly a job for Esperanza. I should have devised a way to put Erick and her together as a bowling duo.

"The last time we played, wasn't Savannah averaging about seventy?" Davis asks Esperanza.

"Worse," Esperanza replies, winking at me. I cannot take my eyes off of Esperanza. She is wearing low-rise boot cut jeans and a turquoise half T-shirt with Assata Shakur's image on it. Her hair is in two curly ponytails. Diverting my eyes away from this forbidden fruit, I attempt to stretch my peripheral vision as far as possible, to stare at her glistening belly without anyone noticing; I want to run my tongue along her four pack of a stomach. She dedicates thirty minutes of core Pilates to her belly each day. My heart pulsates in delight and, for a brief moment, I forget about my teammate. I hug my pink bowling ball to my chest, waiting for Erick to finish with his second turn of the frame. Erick's black scuffed ball finishes his frame by knocking down three out of the six pins he had remaining.

Davis and Esperanza cheer him on with whistles and clapping. I simply respond quietly to myself with a 'this is such B.S.' sigh; a perfect reminder of how much this whole situation sucks.

"Savi, you're up," Davis tells me.

"I know," I say with slight annoyance. Esperanza gives me a curious expression of, 'What's up? Everything okay?' I shrug, amble to the beginning of the lane, and then throw the ball fiercely, pretending that the ivory pins are topped with Erick's face. I get another strike.

"But you suck at bowling! You've always sucked at bowling!" Davis exclaims with his arms up in air, Esperanza jumping up and down clapping for me. Her size C cup breasts bounce up and down in perfect rhythm. I command myself not to become wet.

"Hi five!" Erick exclaims to me as he raises his right palm in the air. *Hi five? Jesus, man, how white can you be?* I reluctantly slap my palm in his hand, and then give him a half smile.

"You really suck at this?" Erick asks me as he picks up his bowling ball. I shake my head, "A lucky streak that shall disappear in a few minutes."

"You're actually beating me! You never beat me!" Davis says to me. I sign back, "Stop being a baby."

Thirty minutes later, we have started a new game, boys against girls. Still, I have not started Erick's lesson. However, he seems to be enjoying himself and has not asked for his formal lesson yet. Perhaps he thinks this is the lesson; that if he hangs around with enough brown and Black folk, his oblivion will magically disappear.

"Is it me, or is it really hot in here?" Davis asks all of us. He takes off his black tee shirt to reveal a sleeveless white tee shirt underneath. I roll my eyes. He has a damn near perfectly muscular body that he will give any reason to put on display. He and Esperanza did track and field in high school together. It was she who introduced him to it. They would do their abs workout several times a week at his house while watching movies featuring *The Rock* for some strange reason.

"Just like I remember," Esperanza tells Davis. Davis grins as Esperanza says, "Let me feel, let me feel." Davis flexes his right biceps and Esperanza wraps her cute fingers around it. Whatever … Yes, I would do anything to be Davis at this very second.

"Sexy," she says. I roll my eyes again, telling myself not to become jealous. She has always found Davis extremely sexy and has shared with me, numerous times, of her fantasies of Davis banging her. During sleepovers, each second of her reveries had been painful for my virgin ears to digest, as I lay underneath the blankets beside her, in her full size bed.

"Well, I'm jealous," Erick comments, implying he wants to be Davis I guess.

"That's because he takes the hormones his family uses on their cows," I tell Erick and Esperanza.

"Hey, he can't hear you," Erick tells me.

"That's the point—"

"What's she saying?" Davis asks, lifting up his head, "'Cause I know she had to say something stupid."

"Nothing," Esperanza tells him.

"Is she lying?" Davis signs to Erick? Nodding, he replies, "I heard something about you using growth hormones." Davis playfully gives me 'the finger' and I whisper, "He's such a hick."

"He does have a nice body," Erick comments.

Whatever …

***

"This lipstick or this one?" Esperanza asks me, an hour later. It is ten o'clock. She and I are at Lotus, a Thai Restaurant, in the lady's bathroom. Esperanza is asking me for beauty tips and I wonder if she is trying to impress Davis, Erick or both. I point the darker color.

"Thanks … What color are you wearing?" She asks me.

"Brown sugar," I slightly mumble, and then pucker my thick lips in the mirror, slit my eyes, and then give myself an air kiss. My eyes then avert to the two-inch scar in the middle of my forehead. *Stupid scar.*

"The cocoa butter isn't working with this scar," I complain to her.

"It's not so bad. I think it's gotten less visible since I first met you. Anyway, why haven't you and Davis hooked up yet? Did you see those arms? He is so damn fine. The boy is 6'4" and huge. I bet his package down there is quite impressive. I wonder what it would feel like—"

"Oh god, stop," I beg, trying not to visualize Davis' "package" while wondering if Esperanza lost her virginity at college.

"I can't believe you're not together yet! You're like a couple, anyway. What's up?" she exclaims. I shrug, "We're platonic. It's just the way things worked out between us. It'd be like sleeping with my brother."

"You do know that you're the only one in the relationship that feels this way? This past week he told me that he's saving his virginity for you but I'm not supposed to tell you." *Hello! What relationship?*

"Bull crap," I respond.

"For the one hundredth time, Davis told me how much in love he is with you. He knows you see him as a brother but he is still hopeful that you will 'come around.'-And who is this Erick? Is he really just a classmate or a possible love interest? He's cute. I'm surprised since he's kind of preppie and all." *Why do you and Davis think I want screw to this shithead?*

I immediately—but kindly—correct her assumption by briefly explaining to her why Erick has entered my life. I don't want her thinking I am still as emotionally aggressive towards white folk as I used to be. I try to make the story sound as if I willingly and optimistically want to help my academic colleague by giving him free lessons about his oblivion to his own white upper-middle class perception of the world.

"Wow, that's a big step for you. I'm sure you'll find you have more in common than you think," she tells me. *I don't think so, hon.* She gets all warm and fuzzy and says, "Oh, I'm so happy for you," and then gives me a long hug. Her soft breasts push into mine and mine into hers. Within seconds, my red thong has turned from a desert to a wetland. *Great, I hate walking around in wet underwear when it's cold out.*

"Why do girls go to the bathroom together and take forever?" Erick asks, when she and I return to our table. The entrees have already arrived and Davis is chomping away at his.

"Your tacky ass couldn't wait for us to come back before you started? You have no class," I reprimand Davis, who is devouring his chicken dish without shame.

"You should wear your hair like that all the time. It's ... cute," Erick tells me. Though I usually straighten my hair with the hot comb, I am wearing a single afro puff for Esperanza.

Esperanza raises her fist in the air and exclaims, "Angela!" then bows her head down dramatically; fist and arm still extended in the air. I shake my head, roll my eyes, and giggle at my spunky friend. The allusion becomes funnier when Erick's eyes meet mine with a look of confusion.

"It's a Black thang," I explain, then sip my Lemongrass soup.

"Half-Black thang for us multiracial folk representin'!" Esperanza pipes, head still bowed down, fist up in the air, giggling. A second later, she lifts up her head to meet the confused uncomfortable eyes of Erick and explains, "My Dad was Nigerian and my mama is Guatemalan and Irish." Thanks to a young horny missionary who couldn't resist doing more than just spreading the word of God to her fourteen-year-old grandmother, who was orphaned at the time.

"Oh. So ...?" Erick begins rather nervously, "Is my tutorial beginning?" I cringe at his choice of the word 'tutorial.'

"I guess." I try to think of what approach to take. Maybe I can tell him to read some bell hooks or something, say twelve hail Marys, then proclaim, 'On this day forward, you are no longer oblivious to your own whiteness.' After all, he thinks I have magic powers tonight as the Magic White-Guilt-Free fairy.

"Well, what do you want to know about?" I ask. He shrugs, "White privilege is a good start. I mean, I know about it, just don't see when I am doing it—or when you say I am doing it. I read that Peggy McIntosh article, but I just don't see how it applies to me. It was written a while ago. Isn't it kind of outdated?"

"What?" Davis asks.

"He wants me to tell him about white privilege," I sign. Shaking his head, Davis turns to Mr. Roberts, "Can I ask you a serious question?"

Erick gingerly sips his mango bubble smoothie and nods.

"Are you on crack or something?" Erick shakes his head and raises a questioning eyebrow.

"Why the hell did you pick Savannah? I mean, honestly, do you know what you are getting into with this bitter Black girl? Don't you understand what her agenda is?" Erick shakes his head, probably wondering if Davis is joking or not.

"To eliminate all white people by 2010."

"Shut up, Davis," I sign.

"I'm just kidding. You know I'm kidding, right?" Davis says to Erick. *You're such a moron sometimes, Davis.* I hope Esperanza is still convinced that I am trying to be good. I shoot her a 'nervous but everything is in control' smile.

"I know you're joking. I take it you are used to her … views?" he replies in Sign and verbally.

"I've been subjected to her 'Kill Whitey' campaign since we were toddlers."

"He's lying. I have never advocated the genocide of any particular population," I say right to Davis with serious eyes that translate into, 'I will cut you if you don't shut up.'

"Her most famous line, 'White people: Can't live with 'em, can't shoot 'em.'" Erick is silent for several seconds. Suddenly, Davis bursts out laughing, "I'm totally joking!" Erick's startled expression turns into apprehensive laughter.

"I have never said that, Davis. Stop it!" I exclaim and sign, trying to control the tone of my voice.

"Davis, you're not helping," Esperanza says. She leans over and steals a piece of fried tofu from my plate, but then redeems herself with a mischievous smile.

"He isn't paying attention," I tell her. Davis turns toward Erick, "But hope is not lost, for I am white and she has befriended me. Theoretically, I guess it is possible for that to happen again. In theory, of course. However, you'll have more of a chance of winning the lotto, second to getting hit by lightening." Erick is laughing again. I do not know what is so funny.

"He's such an idiot," I tell Esperanza, sigh, then continue, "I mean, this isn't even funny," I whine, looking down at my meatless plate, wondering why I ordered a vegetarian egg-free dish just to impress Esperanza. My cranky stomach craves the chicken that is on Davis' green ceramic plate … and *Coca-Cola*.

"Whatever," I whisper to myself, stabbing a piece of tofu with my steel fork, and then smothering it in hot sauce to see if my taste buds will be able to tell that it's not spicy chicken.

Everyone gets to be what he or she wants. These two idiots get to be white clueless men, Esperanza gets to be in Toronto, and what in God's name do I get?

The tofu enters my mouth, and within seconds, I realize that the spicy sauce is far hotter than I had realized it would be. I start coughing uncontrollably and then grab my honeydew smoothie.

Esperanza pats me on the back and asks if I'm okay while Davis and Erick giggle, amused by my situation.

When I'm done coughing up the last bits of killer tofu, Davis shakes his head, and with his right thumb and index finger, he makes the 'L' loser sign on his forehead.

That's what *I* get.

***

We do not leave the restaurant until nearly midnight. I cringe at the fact that I will have to wake up at five in the morning for work. We are all driving in Erick's car. Erick and Esperanza are up in the front. Davis and I are in the back, and I am trying to figure out how I have gotten to this point. Somehow, Davis had ended up doing most of the talking at the restaurant. Esperanza had chimed in a bit while I didn't say anything; just rolled my eyes every other minute and wondered what drugs I had been on when I had agreed to help Erick overcome his oblivion.

"So, I know you said you were doing work at University of Connecticut? What kind?" Erick asks Esperanza. She explains how she has ended up being able to participate in a long symposium and granted temporary junior visiting scholar status at the university, until mid June.

"Wow, you must be pretty smart to get that as an undergrad. So, how'd you meet Savannah?"

"I gravitated to the first Black person I saw when I came to East Lebanon when I was eight. I ended up being in Savi's class. The teacher wanted to pair me up with this little girl who kept on playing with her ponytails and picking her nose. I told her I didn't want to sit next to a *blanquita*, so, I asked to sit with Savannah who was sitting in the back. She was stalking me with her eyes and wearing the most beautiful orange dress—"

"I was not stalking you. I was assessing the new situation," I explain with a smile, remembering that wonderful day of finally seeing such a beautiful golden brown Esperanza Perez enter the classroom.

75

"You called your classmate a blanquita and the teacher didn't get mad at you?" Erick interrupts.

"Paaleease! She had no clue what I was saying. I kind of pretended not to be able to speak English too well just so the teacher wouldn't have to deal with my complaints in a language she didn't understand. I was proficient in English but I knew I could get away with the whole, 'No hablo ingles,' thing." She does not share with him that her two sisters, mother and grandmother are living in North America because their lives had been in danger. Her father had been murdered in Guatemala because they were trying to organize the coffee and cocoa growers to fight for better wages and living conditions.

"Cool," Erick responds, his tone indicating that he wants to dig deeper into why she had chosen to sit next to me rather than a blanquita. With an irritated sigh I think, *Just ask her, you putz.*

I nudge Davis, realizing he has fallen asleep on my shoulder. He's too tall to be in the back seat, however, he had let Esperanza sit in the front since she is tall as well. Sighing, I want to be alone with Esperanza so we can talk. I wonder if she is attracted to Erick. With my luck, probably so.

"So, do you speak a second language?" Esperanza asks him.

"Three, actually. French, German and English. Took a term or two of Spanish. My family and I used to vacation in Austria, Belgium, or France each summer, so I learned that way."

"Are you serious?"

"Yea ... You sound surprised."

"Kind of ... I mean, haven't you heard of the famous joke regarding Americans?"

"No."

"What do you call a person who speaks two languages?"

"Bilingual."

"Three languages?"

"Trilingual."

"So, what do you call someone who speaks one language?" He thinks for several second then shrugs, "I don't know."

"An American."

"That's harsh. We aren't that bad." She giggles and Erick admits, "Okay, maybe we are."

Davis starts snoring. Nudging him again, he does not respond.

"Are you awake back there, Savi?" Esperanza asks me.

"Yea. Davis is snoring, not me."

"I can't believe he found it comfortable enough to fall asleep back there. He's so tall," Erick notes.

"He can sleep on top of broken glass," I say, nudging Davis to remove his heavy head from off of my petite shoulder.

"So, can I call you Savi for the rest of the term?" Erick asks me. No, you can't … I can't wait until I get home.

"Whatever," I reply.

"Her mother calls her Savannah Poo—"

"Esperanza, don't tell him that!" *I don't like Erick. Isn't it obvious Esperanza? Why can't you and Davis see that he's just plan freaking annoying and that I don't want to have anything to do with him!?* My eyebrows furrow and then I sigh loudly in frustration.

"Damage is already done. Next time we get into a class debate, I'll call you Savannah Poo." Esperanza and Erick both laugh. Of course I don't agree with the humor, lay my head back, and then pretend to fall sleep.

***

November 20, 1997
Dear Diary,

I really like Esperanza. Her family is very nice. She lives with her mama, sisters, and her grandmom. Her daddy is gone. She cries about him all the time. That is sad, because she had a daddy and now he is gone. I don't know my daddy, so I am not as sad.

Last week, everyone talked about Thanksgiving in Mr. Peterman's history class. I like Mr. Peterman. He is nice to me. Esperanza got in trouble though. She kept on saying that our textbook is wrong and that Mr. Peterman is a liar. Mr. Peterman gave her a detention then sent her to the principal's office because she says all the Pilgrims were Nazis. Esperanza tells me a lot of things that I do not know are true or not. She says Americans are selfish and ahbliveeus (did I spell that right?) and that is why nobody else in the world likes us. That made me sad. I am not selfish or ahbliveeus (I don't know what that means yet). Tomorrow I will bring an extra Hershey chocolate bar to share with her so she can know that I am not like that.

***

At the blink of an eye, it's seven hours later and I'm back at the register.

"It's always been two dollars and fifty cents," I tell the customer, a woman wearing a tacky sequined sweater with peroxide blonde hair. She puts the box of cookies on the counter, "Are you sure? I bought some here last week and it was two forty." *Yes, loser. By the way, blue eye shadow is so 1987 ... not that I was alive then, but I've seen cheesy 80's movies.*

"It's always been two fifty," I reiterate. *God, the insanity of arguing over ten cents! Can my life possibly get any more superficial?*

Yawning, I look at the time. It is almost time to go to class. She hands me the money, "Are you sure?" I sigh, obviously irritated and ask myself why I always get whiney customers.

"Well, you don't have to be so snippy about it," she tells me. *Screw you.* I bite my lower lip, trying to calm my bitterness. However, as she is exits, I hear her say it. She actually says it. Back turned to me, and without fear or hesitation, it rolls off her tongue and into the air we both breathe.

"Nigger trash."

***

"I had a good time last night," Erick tells me, as soon as I see him enter class. Great, he is under the impression that he is now part of my group of friends. *Please don't sit next to me. Please don't sit next to me.* He sits right next to me. The face and voice of the cunt skank who called me that word this morning still won't leave my ears.

"That's good," I reply, looking over the essay I had to read for class. 'Nigger trash?' I can't believe she said that. *Who is she calling 'trash?'*

"I like your hairdo," he tells me, poking my afro puff with his index finger. Yea, he probably thinks I am doing it for him. I am wearing it for Esperanza, since we will be meeting up later that day. I know he will probably ask me when is the next time we are going out. *Never. You just don't get it, Erick. My friends and I are not exotic novelties.*

"Thanks," I say.

Class starts. The topic of the day is class struggle and if Marxism is useful to understand global poverty. Though I should be debating in class, I am silent. The bitch from the store is still on my mind. She should not be bothering me this much. Why am I not used to the word …? *She is nothing. She is no one. I can't believe she said that. Who the hell does she think she is? She is nothing.*

"Stupid ugly cracker whore," I say in a rather loud whisper. Erick hears me; maybe several others, too.

"Did you just say what I think you said?" he whispers to me.

"No," I lie. Kind of dumb reply since it is obvious I am lying … Who cares? What's Erick going to do about it? Then I start thinking about Esperanza and how much I have missed her; how the love of my life will never be with me.

Class ends several minutes later. My history of South Africa class has been canceled. Sighing, I am now thinking that I have enough free time, until three, to maybe catch up on some more reading … or take a nap in the student lounge. A nap would definitely ease my mind a bit.

"So, what are you up to?" Erick asks me. *You'd think you would get the feeling that I don't like you.*

"Nothing." Swinging my bag over my shoulder, I want to say to him, "Go away."

"Well, can I talk to you for a few minutes?" *He's never going to stop following you. Just nod.* Nodding, "Sure, but let's go to the lounge."

"Cool."

"What's up?" I ask him a minute later, sitting down on the yellow leather couch. My stomach grumbles and the vending machine next to me starts calling my name. Though they hurt my stomach, I could go for some cheese crackers with peanut butter, washed down with a *Coke*.

"This is awkward," he begins. *Hurry up!*

"Okay, here it goes. I really had a good time last night ... Well, I don't usually do this when I first meet someone, but I just gotta ..." he stops himself short, trying to figure out how to say whatever he is going to say. I immediately think, *Great, you're in love with the same girl that I am in love with. Can my life get any shittier?*

"I have a crush. I know I was supposed to be learning last night and not thinking of my romantic life, but it just happened." *Say it. Just say it! Esperanza is your soul mate and you must know more about her and can only do that through me.*

"... And it's just a crush. I'll probably be forced to keep it that way, nothing more, but ... is there any chance that, well ..." *Say it! Ruin my day some more!*

"... that Davis is gay or bi?" Suddenly, my mind is clear of everything that has irritated me in the last six hours. I tell myself not to respond with surprise, but it is difficult, because I am not sure if I have just heard what he said. One thousand questions enter my mind.

Act normal. Don't act as if you're surprised. However, I know the expression on my face has already given it away. Erick grins, "Come on, Savannah. Please don't tell me you don't know that I'm gay." I cannot answer the question. I merely shrug with a slight look of confusion.

"You're joking, right?" My mind begins to race, trying to remember instances from the past seven weeks that may have hinted this. Unfortunately, my mind draws a blank.

"Freaked out that I am not the oppressive white male hetero you may have assumed me to be?" He takes his backpack off, and then turns it around to face me. There are a million skiing buttons on it, however, he points to the pink triangle button in the middle, with a PeTA button next to it.

"Do you know what this means?"

"Kind of," I lie.

"Basically, I'm saying 'I like dudes ... Really like dudes. No closet for this homo!' Well, in a nutshell." I cringe at the word 'homo' and try not to think of myself.

"I've seen the rainbow, before," I say.

"My rainbow button fell off. Anyhoo, now you know ... It can also mean lesbian too, but in black—I mean, the triangle is black—I mean, you don't have to be just a Black lesbian to wear it. It's for all lesbians ..." I cringe again, wondering how he can use the word 'lesbian' so comfortably yet simultaneously find tremendous discomfort in saying the word 'black.'

"You're the last person I'd suspect," I begin, foolishly.

"That's what my father told me just before he threw me out of his house. That was right after I came out to the parents and all in 1999." I feel strange and don't know what to say or how to react. I simply reply with, "Sorry?"

"It's not your fault he's an asshole. So, is Davis at least bisexual?"

"Um, no—I don't know—I guess not."

"Oh well, my gaydar's pretty good but I thought I'd ask anyway. Didn't think he was, but it never hurts to ask. So, you're sure there's no possibility?" Nodding, "Oh yea. I'm pretty sure he only likes girls. He's mentioned many times that he and I should be together."

"That's interesting," he comments. *What? That someone may actually find me sexually attractive? That someone may want to kiss a mouth full of crooked teeth?*

"What?" I ask suspiciously.

"Sorry. Nothing. Thinking out loud. I do that sometimes—"

"What!?" I repeat with annoyance.

"It's nothing, Savannah."

"Say it!" I insist.

"Well, correct me if I'm wrong, but aren't you a lesbi—"

"You're wrong." I don't want to deal with this now ... or ever. I want to get up and walk away, but walking away will make him know that his allegation is correct. He doesn't deserve to know about me that way; in any way.

He thinks for several seconds, reading my face. How can he possibly know?

"Sorry, I didn't mean to put you on the spot. I guess my gaydar's way off. Happens sometimes," he says, his eyes averting away from me. We both feel the situation and air become thick with awkward tension.

"You didn't put me on the spot, but you're wrong," I try to tell him calmly. Standing up, I say, "Listen, I have to go and eat lunch before class starts so ..." Damn it all to hell! ... Everything frustrating in my life comes back into my head in a cacophony of confusion. I turn around quickly, and then put my backpack on.

"Erick, I'll see you in class next week." As I begin to feel my eyes become watery, I hurry out of the lounge.

Never let them see you cry. Then, 'Nigger trash,' starts repeating in the back of my mind again. Simultaneously, I begin to worry about when the emphysema will take Mama away from me ...

... I am crying. Quickly, I wipe my tears away, removing the evidence that life is taking its toll on me. Not feeling like I can walk any further, I collapse onto a bench near a display case featuring the artifacts of a Native American tribes that used to live where Stonehill now stands. *Why did I stay up so late to go bowling? I'm so tired. Everything is messed up.* I put my face in my hands. *Stop crying. You're not weak. Someone might see you, you pathetic piece of crap. Stop crying!*

"Savannah," I hear a familiar voice, several seconds later. It is Erick.

"Go away. Just go the hell away," I mumble. However, he remains there. Finally, I reveal my tear-streaked face to him. He is squatting in front of me with his hands folded, eyebrows crumpled, "Are you okay?" He touches my knee. Suddenly, the hostility I usually feel towards him has vanished. I have finally broken down and the one person I don't ever want to witness it is.

"Come on," he says. Outstretching his arms, my 5'1" body is embraced by the most unlikely of souls.

CHAPTER EIGHT

It is a nice café. I have never been here before because it looks too expensive. The air is filled with pleasant aromas. Green tea, chamomile, peppermint, Ceylon, and other indistinguishable fragrances swirl around in the air.

Erick sits across from me with a cup of tea in front of him. The table is beautifully tiled with reflective mosaic pastels; orange, green, yellow and purple giggle back at me as the sunrays, piercing through the windows, cheerfully dance upon them.

I cannot believe this. I cannot believe this. It is about twenty-five minutes later. Somehow, Erick and I have ended up at Café Blue Serenity, a tea café across the street from the college. I have finally stopped crying and am trying to figure out how Erick has talked me into coming here. My rage towards him is literally gone for the moment. I want to dig deeper into myself to find it because it has to be there somewhere...but, it isn't. I sigh. Perhaps my nervous breakdown has officially started and is short-circuiting my emotions.

Erick sips his peppermint and chamomile herbal tea, and patiently endures my silence, waiting for me to say something. However, I want to keep it inside of me. Looking down at the tea I have yet to touch, I realize that I have never been much of an herbal tea drinker, but Erick claims it will make me feel much better. Finally, I bite the bullet and begin in a low whisper, "How did you know?" *Do I really have 'dyke' written on my forehead?*

"It's not like it was one thing you did or said."

"So, 'loser dyke' wasn't written on my forehead when you first met me?"

He takes a sip from his tea. I nervously start to chew the inside of my lower lip. My heart begins to beat a million miles per hour.

"Why do you use those words? Maybe you can think deeply about why you'd want to refer to yourself in that manner. Does it make you feel good? Does it make you feel sad? You know, think about it for a few minutes." I shrug and sigh. I know he's sincerely trying to help me, but his approach makes me feel like a lab rat being scrutinized by some stuffy white researcher. Why can't he just talk to me without regurgitating everything in Academia that he's ever read?

I merely shrug again in reply to his slightly condescending approach. *Like I don't know how I feel is destructive. Duh!—Okay, he's trying and right now he's probably your only safe door through this whole lesbian thing.*

"So, you do think of yourself as a 'loser dyke,' but you're neutral about it?"

"I guess."

"Do you realize that calling yourself that is a form of internalized homophobia? Why not think about yourself as a 'lovely dyke?'" As the last two words roll off of his tongue they send shivers up my spine. *What is so 'lovely' about being a bulldagger?*

"Don't you think I know this!?" I say rather loudly. Several seconds later, I apologize, "Sorry, I didn't mean it." He smiles and pats my hand, "It's okay, Savannah, I've learned to desensitize myself to your militant behavior." I put my forehead down on the table, "I'm not a militant … How can you live like this without going crazy?"

"Because I'd go even more crazy if I didn't. It's a process. Nine years ago I just wanted to die. But now I can't think of anything else but living!" He says in an optimistic tone, touching the scar on his throat.

"Nine years! That's so long, though," I whisper.

"Relax. It's different for everyone. It took my ex-boyfriend a few months to deal with the whole thing."

"You don't understand," I mumble.

"I do, Savannah. You need to talk to someone or you could end up taking a tragic path."

"Paaleeassse. I'd never think of killing myself, Erick," I lie.

"I was thinking the same thing a week before I overdosed on a lovely drug cocktail at a club at Avalon, in Boston, the week my dad kicked me out of the house."

"Shit, why can't I be normal? I'm Black, female, and poor in America. I think that's about all I can handle." *Right in front of Erick! You just inadvertently admitted to Erick that you have reservations about the cards you've been dealt on all fronts.*

I clench my fists and suddenly start fearing that if I don't stand up and walk away now, I may give Erick the impression that I'm more 'pissed' about being Black than 'proud.' But that's not true. He won't understand. He can't.

"You are normal, Savannah. Contrary to popular belief, there is no normal sexual orientation."

"Whatever ..." I mumble with pure pessimism and a roll of my eyes, "Just like there is no normal class, or race, or whatever. Well Erick, I know you're trying to help, but that's complete horse crap."

"This is going to be a challenge," I hear him mumble to himself.

"You never told me how you knew," I say.

"I have nicely honed gaydar. Years of practice," he says with a smirk.

"Could you possibly be anymore vague?"

"Okay. Well, the most obvious were your interactions with Esperanza. Call me crazy, but I'd say you're in love with the girl."

"Why can't you be this perceptive in class?"

"Are you done?"

"Sorry ..."

"I've caught you taking a second glance at Lily and June's legs when they have worn mini skirts to class. I swear you were staring at Francesca's boobs, the entire class, last month, when she wore that tight red shirt."

"No shit, really?" He nods. I moan, "Oh, everybody must know."

"I don't think so, Savannah. If your best friends aren't aware of it, I don't think your classmates will be. Anyway, who cares if they do? It's 2007, not 1907."

"Well, Davis can't see past his own fantasy of he and I being together. Esperanza told me he's saving himself for me. Do you think Esperanza knows?" Erick shrugs, "Maybe. Obviously, it doesn't seem to bother her since she seems comfortable around you. She's pretty radical anyway, after hearing about the work she's doing in Toronto. Anyway, let's take this one step at a time."

"Take what, 'One step at a time?'"

"Coming out."

"Oh, I don't wanna do that now."

"So, when are you going to deal with it?"

"When I have time."

"You're joking, right?" Shaking my head, "I don't have the time."

"This isn't something you put in your planner, Savannah."

"This is dumb—"

"No, it isn't."

"How would I even begin, Erick? Oh, I shouldn't even be talking to you about this."

"Why not? Is this a racial thing again?" He rolls his eyes and then begins to shake his head. I crumple my eyebrows and shake my head too. He then raises his eyebrows in a *"Well, is it?"* expression, and then starts rotating his 18k gold Harvard class ring around his perfectly manicured and clean ring finger. I think about how embarrassed I am at the idea of even ordering, let alone wearing, a class ring that represents my loser community college.

"No Erick. It's an every thing. Just look where I am from and look where you are from."

"... and?"

"And!? My town is an all white rural town, so it might as well be 1907. There is nothing there. I don't even think there are any 'out' people in my town. You were living in Boston's South End for the past seven years. If I came out, what the hell would I do? I'd still be alone and be called a dyke instead of the n-word. Nothing would change." He finally stops playing with his obnoxiously big gold ring.

"Aren't you exaggerating just a bit?"

"No, I'm not. Some bitch called me the n-word today."

"Like, thee n-word? You're kidding."

"No, so don't tell me I'm overreacting. My life sucks, and I really don't need to add anymore crap to it."

"Calm down ... Sorry." He had been right. This would be a challenge.

***

"Savannah Poo, you're home late two nights in a row," Mama greets me. It is almost midnight and she is sitting at the kitchen table, doing crossword puzzles. I am surprised that she is still up.

"Sorry, Mama. I was at the café with Esperanza," I say. Erick had dropped me back off at school after our little corny therapy session. In the stack of the main library, I had idled up and down the aisles for an hour, trying to peek into the gay book stuff without anyone noticing. I had failed; someone was always there, passing by.

"It's okay, baby. You know I can't set a curfew for you anymore." I greet her with a kiss on a cold cheek. She tries to save us money by turning the heat on only if I am home as well.

"As long as you are safe and having fun, that's all that matters. Let me go and turn the heat up." She leans over to the wall and turns up the thermostat. She seems a little anxious about something. Paranoia immediately sets in; immediately, I too become anxious, wondering if she's figured out why her daughter will never marry Davison Ryan Allen III.

"You're up pretty late, Mama. You feeling okay?" She nods, "I've just been thinking and doing the crosswords a bit." She turns the radio down and clears her throat, "I'm going to go back to work again, starting Monday, since my leave of absence can't be extended, and Uncle Sam ain't gonna give us that pitiful little sick leave money, come Friday."

"Come on, you know you're not strong enough—"

"I'm fine. You shouldn't have to work so hard for the both of us and go to school at the same time … I'm sorry I yelled at you about your paper the other night. I know you haven't had much time to do your homework." Sitting down beside her, "Mama, I don't mind it. Like you said, I'm an adult now. This can be my responsibility. I am handling it just fine," I contest.

"When was the last time you were able to sleep late? And you shouldn't have to work on Saturday either. Your spring break starts next week and I want you to enjoy it like every other kid." She gestures for me to give her my small hands. Extending them out to hers, she squeezes them firmly, and through choked words, whispers, "I want you to enjoy something."

"Mama, I can stop being confrontational with my teachers and give them what they want. Then, they can give me an A and I can get better financial aid next year. Mama, it's okay. I know I complain a lot, but it's okay. I don't need to do the things that all the other kids do for break."

"No Savi."

"I can work for us. I didn't mean for you to go back to work. I knew they wouldn't pay you after tomorrow, that's why I'm working more hours. We can apply for disability. Anyway, I was even planning to take next term off. I'm sorry, please don't do this. You have to get better. You have to rest. You have to heal."

Why did I complain about her food so much this past week!? I shouldn't have done that. Savannah, you selfish loser.

"Poo, it's not that bad. I know you deserve better, but I just have never been able to give you better. Let me give you this. I'm sorry I yelled at you the other night at dinner, but I want you to know that it's not like I never thought you didn't deserve better."

"I didn't mean to complain about the okra. I like your cooking. I do, Mama, I do."

"Poo, it's not about that. I want you to call Kitter and tell him you are taking vacation days for spring break. You should enjoy your break like all the other college kids."

"What if you faint and have to go to the hospital again?"

"If that happens, then it happens." Looking into my mother's eyes, I realize how much this means to her. How can I argue against those eyes? She shrugs within the green, black, and white paisley pajamas she has worn nearly every day, since I can remember. Below the bottom of the pants, she usually wears the red fleece slippers I bought for her from Walmart, four years ago, for her birthday. These are the slippers that always smell like *Virginia Slims*, despite me using the strongest detergent I could find to clean them. Despite the tremendous loss of weight, Mama's ebony colored skin is flawless. She could easily pass for a thirty year old. However, her dark brown eyes tell a different story; the whites of her eyes seemingly looking more yellow, with some redness, every week.

Those eyes look up at my scar. Ebony brown fingers reach out to lightly touch it, "If you ever remember, you'd tell me, right?"

Several times a year, she will ask me this out of the blue. However, ever since she was diagnosed with the 'unwanted house guest,' she's been asking me once a week now, "… you'd tell me, right?"

She focuses back on the conversation, "Call Kitter tomorrow morning, okay? You deserve to have a break, too."

"Okay Mama, I will."

CHAPTER NINE

I don't deserve this, I think, as I listen to a customer talk about nothing. My Saturday shift started about six hours ago. In front of me, is a female customer babbling about God knows what: something about how great the deli sandwiches were at Quikstop this week.

"...and when I say, 'Put a little mustard on it,' he actually knows what I am talking about. And I love how you get a free pickle and chips ..."

Blah, blah, blah, blah ... Kill me.

"...have you ever tried a sandwich from here? I'm sure you have."

"Yes and it changed my life," I reply with dry sarcasm. Of course she probably doesn't even realize I want her to take herself and her sandwich 'to go.'

"I'm going to come here for lunch all the time, now," she tells me. *Yes, because my life couldn't possibly take a turn for the worse.*

Sitting down and closing my eyes, I try to relax a little before the next customer comes to the counter. It isn't even ten seconds that goes by when I hear the entrance bell jingle. Reluctantly, I open my eyes. It is the one and only Captain America.

"What are you doing here?" is my greeting to him. Walking up to the counter, he throws his arms up in the air, "What!? No, 'How are you, Erick?' 'It's nice to see you, Erick?'" Why is he always in such an upbeat mood all the time? However, somewhere, way back in my mind, I'm actually glad to see him...and his *Lacoste* turtleneck sweater that probably costs more than my rent.

"Well, you live in Glastonbury, so it's not like this place is conveniently located next to you, Erick."

"I came to see you."

"You lie."

"No. I did. Honestly. It's a beautiful day. Sunny and warm for a change, so why not take a drive out into the agricultural region of Connecticut?"

"You're serious?" I ask him. He nods, "Of course, Savannah Poo! So, what's up?" I shrug, "Nothing," and then sit back down.

"Come on, it must be interesting working here. You must meet a lot of interesting people." Folding my arms, I respond, shaking my head, "You're clueless."

"You're telling me you've yet to meet anyone interesting?"

"The rednecks around here lack any type of interesting characteristics. Occasionally, a preppie Caucasoid will come through, though," I say with a friendly grin.

"Seriously, though, are you feeling better about the whole 'coming out thing?'" *Why did he have to bring this up again?* The grin melts away from my face. I had been trying to forget about yesterday's temporary breakdown.

"Haven't really thought much about it. I mean, I'm trying not to really think about it too much ... Listen, yesterday was just a weird day. I never act like that—"

"Savannah, it's fine. I will always see you as the bitter young lady that I have come to know."

"I am not bitter. I'm passionate and non-complacent," I try to explain, my bitten down fingernails peeling a *Del Monte* produce sticker from off of the debilitated counter.

"So, what are your plans for spring break?"

"Working."

"Everyday?"

"Not Monday through Wednesday. I'm taking a vacation, I guess."

"Savannah, three days isn't really a vacation now, is it?"

"It is for me, Erick Roberts," I whisper, disappointed that he can't be happy for me. I try not to let it bother me too much, as I've been trying to desensitize myself from his statements these days.

"Well, I have a question for you. I understand if you say no, since you're still in the closet—"

"Shhh, don't say that so loudly!"

"Sorry, this place is packed with so many people. What was I thinking!" he exclaims, as he looks around at the store's desolate aisles.

"Bitch," I mumble.

"Did you just call me a bitch?"

"No." He raises his eyebrows at me, pauses for a moment, then continues, "Anyway, I'm planning to go down to Greenwich Village for part of spring break and was wondering if you'd wanna come."

"What's in Greenwich Village?" Erick's jaw drops, "You poor child." Thinking really hard, I try to figure out if I've ever heard of this place. It does sound vaguely familiar. *If he's condescending like he was about Vail, I'm going to hit him.*

"You've definitely been here too long in farm town. The Village is like one of the largest gay hotspots on the East coast!"

"What are you going to do there?"

"What isn't there to do!? So, you interested?"

"In what?" I ask, looking down, obviously pretending I don't know where he is going with this.

"In coming with me, dork!"

"No, thanks. I really don't think it would be a good idea at this time," I barely whisper. However, my heartbeat begins to increase as I become frightened and exhilarated at that prospect of meeting more people like me.

"Are you sure? I heard a little hesitation there."

"I'm sure." *Why am I so stubborn? No, worse ... I am scared.*

"No, I'm not," I say out loud to myself.

"No, you're not sure?" Erick asks with slight confusion.

"Nothing ... I can't go. Thanks for asking, though." He smiles. For the first time, I notice that it is an inviting generous smile.

"Well, if you change your mind, let me know." Yawning, "Sure, Erick."

"Cool, you guys have *Pez*! Sweet!" Reaching towards the display, he grabs a Spiderman dispenser. Beaming like a five year old, I tell him, "*Pez* makes my throat itch. You're a freak."

"Thanks."

"That wasn't a compliment."

***

Later that evening, I'm sitting in our small living room on my yellow and orange beanbag chair, trying not to fall asleep as I plow through a reading assignment. After five pages, I've retained absolutely nothing. My mind is occupied as usual. For once, however, it's not about the money I don't have or Mama's lungs.

'You're a dyke. You're a pussy loving dyke,' will not stop resonating from the back of my mind. I do not want to address it. I cannot address it. How would I even begin?

"Focus on your studies. You need to do well in your classes," I tell myself. However, it is no use. Closing my book, my eyes stray across the room to our glass coffee table. Crawling to the table, I take a good look at the photograph of my mother at the age of sixteen. The picture has always interested me. In the snapshot, Mama's sister is standing beside her, wearing a short afro and gold earrings. Mama's head is tilted slightly towards her sister and smiling mischievously. I had been three years old when I first asked Mama about the picture. She had replied, "My sister and I on our birthday." That's when I learned that Mama is a fraternal twin. She has never given me the actual name of her sister, so I simply referred to her as 'Auntie Mama Twin.'

Looking more closely at the picture, I try to figure out what is going on in the background. However, much like Mama's past, it is a blur. The portrait is priceless to Mama; a portal into a secret era in her life that I hope to someday be invited into. Everyday, Mama thoroughly cleans the antique silver frame the portrait rests in, losing herself in that snapshot of her younger life for several minutes. I cannot imagine what it would be like to not see my twin sister for nearly twenty years. Sometimes I miss seeing Mama after a mere twelve hours. Closing my eyes, I remember Davis telling me that he has over one hundred people in his family—and that is just in Connecticut and Wisconsin. It must be great to know that you have such an extended family; such a supportive network.

Extended family ... Kinship ... Roots ...

Sliding back onto my beanbag, I hug the picture to my bosom. Lonely for intimacy, Esperanza creeps into my mind, and immediately, I fantasize us cuddling and kissing on the living room sofa. The fantasy lasts a mere fifteen seconds because Mama's cough from the bedroom brings me back to reality. Removing the picture from my chest and holding it in front of my lonely face, I mutter, "A bush loving Black dyke with no money, no extended family, and no love life." I grin back at the picture of Mama and Auntie Mama Twin, as if I am there and know what they're grinning about. Finally, shaking my head, I exclaim to an empty living room, "I'm battin' zero!"

***

Why does it always seem like it is Monday? I think, as Davis parks in the lot. The late winter morning is warm and sunny. Hints of spring have finally decided to bless us with its royal presence. Though it is only fifty degrees, it feels great. Davis is wearing a tee shirt and denim shorts. I've decided to wear a long flowing orange cotton summer homemade dress with white strappy sandals. Once again, my hair is up in an afro puff. I had thought that 'dressing up' would make me feel better. Unfortunately, I have yet to feel anything uplifting from the homemade garment.

"You look so beautiful," Davis signs.

"Thanks." However, I am slightly neurotic about my D cup sized boobs looking too big—especially in tighter, more fitted, clothing.

"Really, you should wear cute clothes like this more often. Girls are lucky they can do that." Shaking my head, I answer back, "Nah, I don't feel like putting myself on display all the time. I feel weird today anyway, dressing like this—Stop looking at me that way!" I say, and then zip up my spring jacket.

"What 'way?' What am I supposed to do? You look very good today. You're a pretty girl. What's not to look at!?" He says to me, rolling his eyes and shaking his head in disbelief.

"Whatever," I mouth to him. I have seen this look on his face before, know what will follow, and I attempt to leave the car before he bombards me with it.

"Why don't you ever think you're beautiful?" he signs. I sigh and then shake my head, "Because I'm not, Davis." *I'm not.* My tongue slides along my embarrassingly crooked teeth. *That ugly scar on my head and my big ass nose.*

"So, even though Esperanza and I tell you that you are pretty, you refuse to see it?"

"You don't understand. I don't want to talk about it. So you and Esperanza 'think' I'm pretty. That's two people. Anyway, I have to go to class."

"You know, this messed up way you have of looking at yourself is whacked. You could have any man you wanted if you just changed your attitude." Rolling my eyes, *Here it comes …*

"You know how I've felt about you—feel about you—"

"—STOP!" I sign angrily, reaching for the door handle. *Not now. Not ever …*

"Savannah, don't leave." Sighing, I turn my head back to him, "What do you want from me?"

"I want you to listen to me. You never listen to me about this."

"I do, Davis. I've just yet to give you the answer you are looking for." *Tell him, Savannah. Tell him why it will never happen.*

Having had tea with Esperanza the other night, she had told me that Davis had spoken to her again about his feelings for me, and how he is ready to talk to me about us again. But, how can I explain this to him? This is going to go on forever if I don't do something. *Tell him. Tell him—*

"We get along so well. We enjoy each other's company and have gone through everything together. Everything," he says, sliding his index finger along the scar on my forehead.

"What else could be more perfect? My family loves you. You know my mother loves you. Your mother likes me … This is so frustrating."

I take Davis' hand, command myself to be calm and respectful of his feelings, and explain, "Davis, I love you dearly as a best bud but I can't—I just don't—feel the same way towards you. You've always felt like a brother to me; nothing more. You're my best friend and I am being honest with you."

He nods with a blank face, disappointed and slightly shocked that I had not proclaimed my love for him in the way that he probably had anticipated. Looking down at his hand that I'm holding, he decides to carefully retract it, and then whispers, "Okay." I wait for him to say more, but he doesn't. Instead, he lifts his head up and shrugs nonchalantly. Squeezing his shoulder, I promise, "Listen, we'll talk more, later. I have to get to class."

"Okay," he repeats. He tries to smile, but I can see that I may have broken his heart beyond repair. It's one of the most awkward moments between us in a very long time—well, minus the time, after watching a movie in his bedroom, he suggested we practice trying out "safe sex" with the condoms he bought from *Quikstop* during the week we learned about sex education in health class. We were in the eighth grade.

I bite my lower lip, contemplating doing something extreme, like spontaneously acting straight by French kissing him on the lips. Could I actually do it? Could I pretend to be a straight girl and be with him in that way? Maybe I could learn to pretend. He would be happy while heterosexuality would be my alibi. No one would ever think I am the other way. Maybe I could learn to be happy the straight-acting way. Maybe I could learn to like it.

Both of us sit in the car for a minute or two, silent, not looking at each other, as I emotionally battle the possibility of going through life as a rather convincing straight-girl actress, worthy of receiving a Tony or Academy Award for my performance. *Oh man, I could do it. I know everything about being straight. Seriously, what the hell do I really know about being a lesbian? Being a straight girl, yes. I could pull it off. Mama would be so happy that I married him. She loves him so much. Then we'd be part of their big family and Mama and I would never be alone. Everyone would be happy. Maybe it wouldn't be so bad, as long as he loves me.*

Between the two of us, he is the first one to find the courage to break the silence with, "Sorry ... Just go to class. I don't want you to be late, Savi." He is looking down at his lap, still. I don't want to leave, but he is right, I am late for class and we can always continue this later. I take a deep breath, and then nudge him to look up at me; at least give me a goodbye hug like he usually does. Instead, he turns his head to the driver's side window, and through gritted teeth, but a calm voice, says, "Savi, please just go to class. I'll see you after school," and ends it with a long drawn out and hopeless sigh.

"Goddamit, Davis. If only you knew how much harder it is for me!" I exclaim to his turned head, my voice in a half angry and half miserable tone. Upon speaking to a guy that can't hear me, I suddenly realize that my proclamation has made me feel slightly better. His head still turned, patiently waiting for me to exit the car; I decide to continue with my soliloquy. I do it to feel better and to stop convincing myself of this ludicrous notion of performing a life that is not me.

"I don't dream of being with you, but with Esperanza, the love of my life that I can never be with. I love you so much Davis as the brother I never had, and I wish you could so love me back that way. I'm just scared to tell you the truth because I'm scared that you won't want to be friends anymore." My heart is racing a million miles per hour, exhilarated that finally, I'm speaking the truth; temporarily liberating this weight off of my slender shoulders. It feels so great. God, it feels so unbelievably great to finally tell him what I have wanted to for so many years. This is truly a soliloquy, literally falling on deaf ears. However, I feel relieved for the moment, grabbing the handle of the car door.

I hop out of the car and then slam the door, hoping the vibration will get his attention that I have left. For a finale I wave goodbye, regardless if he cares to look at me or not. Walking towards the college, I decide to turn around fifteen seconds later. Davis is still in the car; his face is covered with his left hand. I take a few steps towards the car as Davis reveals his face again. His strong hands begin wiping tear-laden cheeks. It is the first time I have ever seen Davis cry since we became teenagers.

As I'm quickly thrown off of my high horse, I resist the temptation to run back and comfort him. Shamefully, I hurry to my class.

***

"He's got a PhD in social theory. Obviously, he knows what he is talking about," Lewis Starkley argues with me.

"He's used in academia because he's a white know-it-all male scholar—"

"It's always race, isn't it, Savannah?" Lewis interrupts, sarcastically, rolling his eyes. Ignoring him, I continue, "We've never even discussed the word 'theory' and how something becomes a theory. People have been taking this man's word as if it were the Bible, never questioning his methods or his biases—"

"So, if we had read a theory by say—a Chicana female who never attended college, you'd agree with her?" Professor Rogards asks me.

"It's not about agreeing. It's about why do we take what some people say as if it were etched in stone, while other's aren't taken seriously at all? How do we even really study social theory if the definition itself marginalizes that part of the population that isn't white; that isn't male; that wasn't educated at a top twenty university?" I ask.

"It's not about race," Lewis repeats.

"Yea, it's also about gender, nationality, and class as well," Joan says.

"Professor Rogards, this is ridiculous," Lewis says.

"Lewis is right. Can't we for once just look at the good side of someone's theory?" Lois says.

"Folk, what Ms. Sales is suggesting isn't ridiculous at all. Just because his theory has been used extensively, doesn't mean that it should be taken as the only truth and never questioned. Savannah and Joan bring up valid points within the realm of research: accountability and responsibility. Furthermore, there are thousands of people with superb ideas and theories. However, because they simply don't have a college degree—or if they don't have a degree that is from the global North—they rarely are respected in the Western academy. Furthermore, their knowledge is usually not part of mainstream university curriculum, here in the USA. Of course, this doesn't mean you shouldn't study Darwin or Derrida, but you should realize they do have certain prejudices and preconceived notions just like most of us. On the flip side, just because we read Arundhati Roy for next week, doesn't mean we should only believe her because she is speaking from the global South; she will have biases as well.

However, everyone can learn from even those we think we have nothing in common with ..."

At the end of class, as I shuffle my stuff together, Erick leans over and taps me on the shoulder, "So, what's up?"

"Not much. Was thinking of getting some grub."

"You wanna do lunch or something?"

"Sure." *Wow, you didn't even have to think about it ... You're losing your belligerence, Savannah.*

"Got any preference?" He asks me.

"I've got four dollars in my wallet." Mama's co-payments for her medicine are breaking the bank account.

"Savannah, can I talk to you for a second? Sorry to interrupt, Erick," Professor Rogards asks me.

"That's okay," Erick and I say in unison. "I'll be right outside the door, okay?" Erick tells me. Rogards sits beside me, holding a manila envelope in his hands with a raised eyebrow, "What are your plans for this summer?"

***

Erick steals a French fry from my carton, "What else did he say? I want all the details." Sitting at McDonald's, I am trying to tell Erick the good news, as he looks through the materials Professor Rogards has given me. Though Erick has 'issues' with fast food restaurants, he drove me to my fast food sanctuary, anyway. Less than fifteen minutes ago, my future had been given a glimpse of hope; of potential. Right now, I am waiting for my bedroom alarm to go off and wake me up out of this dream. *I don't think anything good has happened to me all year so this has to be a trick! At any moment I am going to wake up, I just know it!*

"Hey, don't get ketchup on it! I thought you didn't like this stuff anyway? Saying it's all nasty and stuff!" I exclaim to him, as he reads, chomping on a stolen French fry.

"Chill, I see the ketchup. I'm entitled to one French fry. I'm hungry too and all they had here was iceberg lettuce salad for us healthy vegetarians to eat."

"Food snob! Don't ruin it, hypocrite!"

"You need to calm down. It's fine ... Hey, look, you get to stay in a one bedroom apartment single at Columbia! I'm totally visiting! Wow, a free Metro Card! They're even giving you a really generous stipend. All you have to do is basically pay for meals— wait, you have a dining pass for twenty-one meals per week in the university's dining hall. This is so awesome!—And I'll be in New York, like, every other weekend too. I should give you, like, the addresses of some of friends there—"

"I haven't thought about it, yet, Erick. This research assistantship is a lot of time away from home. I have to think about it."

"What do you mean you have to think about it!? Rogards just offered you a chance to work in New York City with free room and board and a stipend! Do you know how prestigious it is to be the research assistant to a McEnroe Fellow at Columbia University? Number one, this fellowship is usually given to a professor at a well-known four year liberal arts college, not a community college like Stonehill—"

"Well, not everyone can go to Harvard, snob, and we're ranked in the top fifty best two year colleges in the country," I spout, opening up my box of Chicken McNuggets.

"I can't believe you're so skinny and eat like that. What do your arteries look like?"

"Eat like what? It's all white meat. It's healthy." He rolls his eyes, "Certainly not healthy for the chickens that had to die for it. I'm surprised you don't care about that since you're all into social justice and stuff." I simply sigh in annoyance and then roll my eyes, choosing to ignore his assessment of my meal. He continues, "You're a teenager, so I know I'm not going to convince you that you can't live off of soda, Dunkin Donuts, and McDonalds for the rest of your life. It's taxing on the immune system." I roll my eyes again, thinking of how I've already heard this spiel from Esperanza, plenty of times.

"Anyway, as I was saying, this research assistantship is usually given to a senior to pursue post-baccalaureate work during the summer; and number three, NYC! You'll never be bored! No cow-town for three months!" Covering my face with my hands, I moan at the word 'cow,' as it reminds me of Davis and how I must talk to him tonight. *What am I going to say? How will I even begin?* The image of him crying in the car has entered my mind again.

"What's wrong?"

"Nothing ... I have a headache," I lie. Uncovering my face, I look directly into his eyes and mumble, "I can't do this."

"Do what?"

"I just can't do this."

"The McEnroe?" Shaking my head then putting my arms up in the air, "Everything! I just can't do it. What am I thinking!? What was I thinking!?"

"What are you talking about?"

I can't go to New York for the summer ... I can't talk to Davis and tell him the truth ... I can never be who I really am, "Ugh, I just can't do any of it ... Who am I kidding?" *What would Mama say? Oh my god, what if she stops loving me? Would she do that? Erick's dad did that to him.*

"You're losing me—"

"Don't worry about it," I sigh, grabbing the McEnroe Fellowship pamphlets from his hand, cramming it back into the manila envelope, and then stuffing it into my backpack.

"I'm not even going to bother reading it. I freaking can't go to New York," Mama can't be home alone. She just can't ... Closing my eyes tightly and clenching my fists, I want to cry again. Yes, it is a cruel trick. The gate to happiness is right in front of me, but they've handed me a bent key. *This sucks. I can't even do it. I can't leave Mama alone ... I shouldn't blame her. I can't blame her. She can't help it that she's sick ... Jesus, what am I going to say to Davis tonight? I can't tell him I'm a dyke.*

"Are you okay?" Erick interrupts. Opening my eyes and unclenching my fists, I search for a lie, "Sometimes I get these really bad migraines and feel so ... immobilized. I can't do anything until it passes. I'm okay, now."

"I think you're just too stressed out. Also, this comfort junk food, and all that coffee you drink, doesn't really help a migraine, you know—"

"I can't help it."

"I know, but there are ways to relieve it. You don't have to be stressed out all the time. Like perhaps taking a short vacation would help. Are you still not interested in going to Greenwich Village with me?"

"That'll just make me more stressed out ... I have to stay here."

"It will only be for a two or three days! Seventy-two hours, tops!"

"I just can't."

"Think about it some more." I simply nod and promise I will, so he can just shut up about that damn stupid idea.

"Okay ... I got something for you," he tells me, lifting up his backpack and pulling out several literature materials and two DVD sets.

"What's this?"

"Pamphlets on lesbian stuff."

"That's okay. I don't need it."

"It's interesting stuff and a copy of the first and second season of the L-Word. I burned you mine.

"Come on, put that away. People are going to see that."

"They can't see this from here." Looking around, I hope no one is looking at our table. Of course, Mr. Oblivious continues, ignoring my pleas for privacy.

"This one's about 'Coming Out,' this one's about safe lesbian sex—"

"Stop, please."

"And homophobia—Oh, and this is about same-sex couple's legal rights in the state of Connecticut—"

"Can't we have one conversation without you bringing this up!?" I exclaim, grabbing the pamphlets and DVD then shoving them into my backpack.

"Okay, Savannah-Poo, we won't talk about this anymore as long as you don't bring race into everything."

"That's not the same thing," I pout. Shaking his head and grinning, "Sometimes your anger in that petite little frame of yours makes you too cute. Just read the stuff and watch the DVDs, okay?"

Suddenly, the strangest sensation comes over me. It feels as if someone is looking at me intensely. Turning around, I try to find where these eyes are coming from.

"Who are you looking for?" Erick asks. Shrugging, "I don't know."

"You're strange."

"You're one to talk." However, I continue to feel as if I'm being watched. Perhaps I am just being paranoid, thinking that everyone has seen the pamphlets and is thinking shit about me.

"So, have you thought about who you are going to tell next?" Erick asks me.

"Tell who what?"

"Hello, what are we talking about?"

"Oh, that …" I turn around again to find where the eyes are coming from.

"Looking for no one again?" I barely hear him ask. My brain registers the question rather slowly and doesn't answer to about five seconds later.

"Someone's looking at me," I allege, my eyes squinting with sternness.

"Who?"

"I don't know. It just feels like someone is looking at me."

"Savannah, you're being too paranoid."

"You can never be too paranoid. Let's go, this is weird."

"Don't avoid the question."

"What question?"

"Coming out. Have you thought about who you are coming out to next?"

"No, I don't want to. Who says I have to tell anyone?"

"So, how the hell is this benefiting you?"

"That's a stupid question."

"No it isn't."

"Erick, come on. You make it sound so easy. You were living in Boston. East Lebanon and Boston are like night and day. I wouldn't even have a gay community to come out to, here. I'd just be a walking target for the town rednecks during hunting season."

"Jesus, you don't have to tell everyone. Your parents and your best friends are good for starters. They wouldn't tell anyone."

"I can't. I wouldn't even know where to begin."

"You say, 'Mom, Dad—'"

"It's just my mama and I—"

"Okay, 'Mama, I'm a lesbian, let's talk." *Verbatim from one of those pamphlets. He's so predictable ... Loser.*

"Don't be so loud," I plead.

"I'm not." *Someone's watching me.*

"Come with me to the Village."

"No." I stand up quickly, startling Erick, then look around me once again. People are watching me. *I wonder if they know? They saw the pamphlets. They all know—*

"Are you okay?" he asks. It sounds like he is far away. My eyes look everywhere. The old white man sitting next to us; the four teenagers standing near the bathroom doors; the three white young women sitting in the booth, chattering about a fashion magazine in their hands; the old couple munching on fries, several feet away from me. Suddenly, they are all looking at me. I know they are looking at me. *They all know what I am and they all hate me. They don't even know me and they all hate me ... Well, I hate them too. I hate every single one of them—*

"Savannah," Erick says to me again. Without answering, I bite my lower lip, shake my head, and then leave McDonald's ... Don't quite know where I want to go. I don't really care. 'Don't bother looking around. If I do, I'll see them staring at me. Like they always do. As if they've never seen a Black lesbo before. I want to go home and hide and never leave again. I don't want to give them anything to look at, anymore—

"Savannah, watch out!" I hear Erick yell out of nowhere. My head shoots up. Suddenly, I realize that the sidewalk I have been furiously walking down has turned into an intersection. Cars and trucks are honking their horns and I hear tires skid. Slightly incoherent, someone pulls me back by my arm back onto the sidewalk, a pickup truck racing by where I had been standing a second ago.

"What are you trying to do!? Are you okay!? Are you crazy!?" Erick asks. I turn around and face him, a genuine look of concern on his face meeting my eyes.

"What are you doing?" he repeats.

"I don't know yet."

"Jesus, please don't ever do that again. I thought you were going back to the car or something."

"Take me back to Stonehill, please."

"Hello! Don't snap at me! You almost got hit by a truck!"

"I know what I am doing. I'm always in control, okay?" I start walking back towards the parking lot and refrain from apologizing to him or even thanking him for pulling me out of harm's way. I don't want him thinking I need him; that I am dependent on him. I don't need him. I don't need no one.

CHAPTER TEN

"So, are we going to talk?" I sign to Davis. As usual, we are sitting at Violet's. He had picked me up without saying anything but a quick sign of 'Hello.' I wonder if he knows I had seen him crying in the car. I wonder if he hates me.

"So, how is this benefiting you?" I hear Erick echoing in the background.

"He's your best friend, Savi," I whisper to myself several times.

"So, are we going to talk for real? This is really important to me," Davis finally says to me. I have figured out how I will tell him. Before he had picked me up, I had written a five-page letter to him, telling him everything; how much our friendship means to me; my feelings for Esperanza as well as my attraction to other girls he has known. Call me a coward, but it's the only way I can do this without having a nervous breakdown.

Sighing, I look out onto the rolling hills of East Lebanon. So much empty space. Nothing to hold onto or to grasp. *Please God, don't make me live here all my life.*

"Savannah, please listen to what I need to say." Stop him now. Give him the letter. It's the only way he'll stop. I laugh nervously to myself, trying not to cry, wishing the truck had hit me.

I am about to give him the letter when a voice screams in my head, "What are you crazy!? Stop! You're not in a city where you can blend in. What difference will it make if you let people know? Let Davis know? Either way you'll still be miserable—more miserable—and stuck in this place for the rest of your life with no Esperanza to love. He'll be at a big university in the fall. He'll find someone special to fall in love with and forget all about his ridiculous fantasies!"

Either way, whether he knows or not, he will never have me. We'll both still be miserable.

Covering my face, I shake my head and tell myself not to cry; not to think about my desolate future; not to think about how I cannot accept the opportunity to do research in New York. *He's leaving for*

Wisconsin at the end of August. Doesn't he understand he'll find the perfect girl? Unlike me, he will not be lonely forever.

Davis wraps his fingers around my small wrists, "Savannah, are you okay? You're shaking." I do not want to look at him. I cannot look at him. Realizing my palms feel wet, I think, *Damn it, I'm crying. Stop crying, Savannah.*

He tries to pull my hands away from my face. I resist and he pleads, "Come on Savannah, stop. What's wrong?" Finally, I let my hands drop, revealing my miserable tear stained face to him. He has not seen me cry for nearly a decade.

Sniffing, I mouth, "I'm sorry." He let's go of my wrists. Signing, I tell him, "I can't love you the way you want me to." Biting his lower lip, he tries to figure out how to respond. The silence between us begins to make me feel even more uncomfortable. I am about to cry again when Davis nods and says, "Let me take you home—I'll just take you home. Yeah, I'll take you home." Standing up quickly and putting his jacket on, he repeats that he will take me home, trying to avoid eye contact with me. His bottom lip is quivering, and I know if he looks directly into my eyes, he will surely cry as well.

***

Sighing, I watch as Davis drives away. It is ten minutes later and I am standing in front of my apartment building. *Everything's gonna work out. Everything has to work out. Tomorrow I am going to wake up and everything will be okay. I just need to go to bed and relax,* I tell myself, wiping my eyes with the cuff of my jacket. I don't want Mama to see that I have been crying.

"I'm home. Early, for once!" I exclaim, as I unlock the door. Sniffing, I wait for Mama to reply.

"Hello?" I say, taking my backpack off and then putting it on the kitchen table. I poke my head into our bedroom to see if she is asleep. She is not there.

Tonight is not Scrabble night, is it? I check the refrigerator for a message. Nothing. The answering machine is blinking. I press play, "Hey Savi, it's me, Esperanza. Spring Break for you next week, right? I wanted to know if you were interested in going to the thrift store with me on Friday or Saturday. We can try on halter-tops together, then go out to a club and entice all the lovely boys. Give me a call … Savannah, it's Erick. Just calling to see if you're feeling any better. Sorry if I put you on the spot at McDonald's. I didn't mean to get you upset or anything. I'm just trying to help because I know how hard this is. Call me if you wanna talk …" I open the refrigerator to get some iced tea, continuing to listen to the answering machine, "Savannah Sales, this is Dr. Raye from Windham Hospital. It is about three in the afternoon, Monday. Your mother was brought through our emergency room about twenty minutes ago …" I close the refrigerator door quickly, rush to the machine, and then turn the volume up, ."..please come down as soon as possible. Also, I can be reached at 860-456-8767." I remain standing, frozen, waiting to wake up.

No, this can't be happening. This absolutely cannot be happening … This isn't happening. Wake up, Savannah—

—The phone rings. My heart is beating a million miles an hour. Closing my eyes tightly and biting my lower lip, I refuse to answer it as it rings again. What if it is Dr. Raye? What if he tells me she's … she's—

—I won't even think it. I do not even want to think of that very thought.

The phone continues ringing.

Answer it … I don't want to. I can't …

The answering machine picks up, "Hi Savannah. It's Professor Rogards. I wanted to give you my cell phone number in case you need to ask me questions about the McEnroe. I won't be in my office much during spring break. 860-537-9876. Don't hesitate to call me. Have a great break, kiddo. You're an amazing young intellectual and I hope we can work together this summer."

Sitting down at the kitchen table, I want to start crying, but I can't. Got no more tears left for the day. I don't want to call this Dr. Raye. He will not have good news for me. Good news does not come my way. Sure, the McEnroe had seemed like good news at first, but it too will end badly. Laying my head down on the table, I close my eyes again and wonder if I can wish it all to disappear.

Drip … drip … drip.

The faucet. The goddamn endlessly leaking faucet.

Drip … drip … drip.

I'm so tired … I'm so freaking tired … and alone. Always alone … Tired …

Drip … drip … drip.

Alone … Tired … Lonely …

"Savannah?" It is the voice I have known since I was a toddler. I do not want to lift my head up and open my eyes. It is too good to be true. I must be dreaming. Why would he come back here?

"Savannah," he repeats. I slowly open my eyes and raise my head. My best friend is standing next to me with his hands in his pockets. Jesus, I had been so tired I hadn't even locked the front door.

"Hi," I say. He sits down, looking at me intensely, signs, "Are you okay?"

"Yes."

"You're a terrible liar." Folding his hands and clearing his throat, "I shouldn't have driven off like that."

"It's my fault. You had every right to leave," I sign to him.

"No, I shouldn't have … You never cry. Not in front of me. Not like that. Not ever. Something is wrong."

"I'm just not attracted to you," I begin to sign.

"Forget that, Savannah. I don't care about that right now. Forget about that and talk to me for real. You looked like you were about to have a nervous breakdown. Something is wrong and like a dumb ass, I just realized this five minutes ago. I promise you, nothing you say could ever ruin our friendship. If that's why you haven't been able to talk to me, I want you to know that I could never leave you for any reason."

"Promise?"

"Cross my heart and hope to die …," he signs back with a sincere smile, "… stick a needle in my eye," he finishes with a whisper. He pulls up Mama's chair, sits down beside me, puts his arm around my shoulders, and then draws me close.

We sit in silence for several minutes as he respects whatever time it takes for me to start talking again. Sighing, I tell myself, *I can do this*, reach over to my backpack on the table, and then stick my hand into my bag. The moment of truth … Do or die.

With a deep breath I hand him the letter I had written him, along with one of the pamphlets that Erick had given me.

CHAPTER ELEVEN

As I look at the picture of Mama and Auntie Mama Twin, I slide my finger slowly across the picture of Mama's young and happy looking teenage face. Laying the picture on my lap, I turn and look back at Mama, sleeping peacefully on the white hospital bed; a Mahogany angel wrapped in white, dying slowly. Quietly.

I cannot remember the ride over here or exactly what Dr. Raye had said to me once I arrived, only that Mama would be okay … for now. She had hyperventilated at work today, after walking up the stairs carrying four reams of paper from the school's storage. Becoming light headed at the top of the stairs, she lost her balance and fell down the stairs. No broken bones, just a mild concussion and bruised ribs. God, she was lucky. She had been hyperventilating more frequently than usual, this past week, despite her anticholinergic and bronchodilator medication. However, she didn't want me to know, so kept it to herself, hoping it would go away.

Davis has gone to the cafeteria for coffee. I am not sure how long he has been gone. I am not really paying much attention to anything except Mama's face and the framed picture in my lap. I don't know why I had brought the picture. I don't even remember grabbing it, but there it is, in my lap.

Davis enters through the curtain opening, holding two cups of coffee in his hands, "I tried to diversify how we drink coffee, and got two Vanilla Hazelnuts instead of regular boring plain coffee."

"Caffeine is caffeine to me … Thanks."

"Careful, it's hot." I nod, setting the cup down on the metal stand next to me, sigh, and then sign, "I hate hospitals." I hate my life. I hate everything …

"Mama Sales is going to be all right. Just relax. I've had a concussion before," he says, putting his hand on my shoulder, "She's going to be okay." He does not know that she has emphysema because I had asked that I speak to Dr. Raye in private, to respect Mama and my promise to not let anyone know. However, in that moment, I feel that I am no longer able to hold on to this emotionally and spiritually draining secret. I let out a long sigh.

"She has E-M-P-H-Y-S-E-M-A," I sign. He crumples his eyebrows in surprise and confusion, "But I thought you said Dr. Raye told you she hit her head?"

With a miserable expression, I reply, "She was diagnosed with it, months ago. That's why she fell down the stairs. She got light headed."

"Let's take a walk," he signs to me.

"I want to stay here—"

"Just fifteen minutes, Savannah. We've been here for three hours. You need a break. She'll still be here ... We can let our coffee cool down."

"Where are we going to go?" I ask, standing up reluctantly with the picture, hugging it like a fragile newborn kitten.

"You can leave the picture."

"What?"

"Leave the picture ... Give it to me." I slowly hand it to him.

"It'll be here when you get back, too. How about we put it right here," he says, placing it on the metal stand so it is facing Mama's sleeping face.

We walk through the halls for several minutes without saying anything.

"Let's go through here," Davis finally says, opening the door to the fire escape stairwell. I hesitate and he says, "Come on. People are lazy as hell and only use elevators. It's nice and private in here." Several seconds later, I am sitting on a step and Davis is sitting across from me on the floor.

"So, let's talk about this," he begins, pulling the folded lesbian information pamphlet out of his front pocket. At the kitchen table, we didn't talk about it. Five seconds after revealing it to him, I had panicked, once again, and told him that Mama was in the hospital and I needed him to take me there.

Unfolding the pamphlet, he reads the title, "Coming Out: Dealing with lesbian sexuality as a teenager ... Like, you're for real about this?"

"Uh-huh."

"No shit, really?"

"Yea. Sorry."

"You don't have to apologize to me. So, you're this way?" he exclaims again, shaking his head in disbelief.

"I'm that way ..." An awkward silence follows between him and me . I am nervous as he reads something on the pamphlet.

"So, like, how long have you, well ... felt like this?" Shrugging, I sign, "Since I was maybe ten or eleven ..."

"Wow. I don't get it ..."

"What?"

"Why did you wait until now to tell me? You didn't actually think I was going to hate you, did you?"

"Maybe ..."

"Don't be dumb."

"You don't have the least bit of hate—"

"I'm a little upset that you waited until you were about to have a coronary before telling me this—and about Mama Sales. What, were you just going to keep it a secret until you went crazy?"

"No ... I don't know. I'm in denial. I don't know. You know how East Lebanon is. They ran those two gay guys who were living together out of town. They fired Coach Nielsen when some stupid parent learned that she was a lesbo."

"Nielsen was fired for coming in drunk all the time. That lesbian story was made up. I thought you knew that. It was a rumor some bored kids started. Mr. Landis is gay, and no one's fired him. You know, our old math teacher from elementary school?"

"He is? No he isn't—"

"Believe me, he is—"

"You're lying." Shaking his head, "You can be so thickheaded sometimes. What reason do I have to lie to you?"

"Sorry." He continues reading the next page to the pamphlet then asks, "You ever do anything with any chicks?" I shake my head.

"Does your mother know?" I shake my head again.

"You gonna tell her anytime soon?"

"Maybe." He pauses, thinking for a second, "How sick is she?"

"Sick enough. Stage 4 emphysema." I tell him how she hasn't worked in over a month; that is why I have been working like the devil at Hellstop. He shakes his head and closes his eyes, "Savannah,

I just don't understand you. You know you could have asked my family for financial help and we would have gladly given it to you. What are you trying to prove?" Opening his eyes, he waits for my reply. Signing, I tell him, "I thought I could handle it. I am handling it. We'll be fine as long as I don't go back to school until spring 2008."

"Don't do this …"

"Don't do what?"

"Drown in your pride, Savannah! Contrary to the American Dream fantasy, no one does it alone. No one makes it alone. My folks sure as hell didn't become successful farming hicks by pulling themselves up by their bootstraps. I know it and I know that you know it, Savi. You are going back to school next term."

"Who else is going to take care of Mama? I'm Mama's only family."

"Savi, you have us."

"What?"

"You have us … You are family. Who says family has to be blood? It doesn't. You and Mama Sales are part of the Allen family. Why do you think whenever we used to go to the store when we were younger, my mom always gave both of us money to buy candy or ice cream? Why do you think you and your mother have spent just about every Christmas Eve dinner at our house?" He grins and finishes, "And why do you think I've been hauling your bratty arse to everywhere you've wanted to go, for the past few years because you can't pass your driving test? I wouldn't do it for anyone I didn't consider family! I don't even charge you for gas!"

Sniffing, I sign in reply, "Sometimes I don't understand myself, or why I do the things I do … and why I can't break out of it."

"That makes two of us …" I explain to him my rationale for not having asked anyone for help; that I honestly think the only person I can depend on for sure is me; that he and his family shouldn't be responsible for us or see us as a burden, since his parents already have five children to worry about.

Davis slides up to where I am sitting, and then puts his arm around my shoulder. Sighing in unison, we remain silent for a while. Closing my eyes, I lay my head on his shoulder.

"Thank you for still loving me," I whisper.

CHAPTER TWELVE

"Let me get that for you, Mama Sales," Davis says, as he pulls the chair out for Mama at our kitchen table. It is Thursday evening. Mama has just been released from the hospital. I have not been home since Tuesday night, and want to take a shower and sleep for eight hours. The last two days have been fuzzy, and the last thing I clearly remember is talking to Davis in the stairwell. I nearly forgot that Saturday is March 24, my nineteenth birthday.

"Mama, I'm going to put this right here in the living room, okay?" She nods with a weak smile as I lug the two small extra oxygen tanks to the side of the television. Davis lugs over the other two. As I stare at our new shiny metallic tenants, I recall Dr. Raye's stoic detached words to me, "Her scans and tests show that she has stage four emphysema. She's now at the stage in which she'll need to have oxygen handy and eventually will need it permanently." *God, he doesn't even care about her. About my Mama, I had thought.* He had never once made contact with my eyes while talking, his tone conveying annoyance because we didn't have "better health insurance" and that Mama "should not have been smoking so much for such a long time" and "someone from her generation should have known better." Mama confessed to him that she had not stopped smoking and was sneaking them in while I was away at school or at work. Thankful that she hadn't died falling down the stairs, I have chosen to hold off on scolding her for lying to me about having quit.

"Want anything to drink or eat?" Davis asks her. She pats him on the cheek and replies, "That's okay sweetie. I just wanna sit here for a few minutes, then go to bed … Help yourself though. There's okra and fried chicken leftovers somewhere in the fridge."

"You don't have to tell me twice. You know how much I love your cooking. Savannah you want me to make you a plate?"

"No thanks. I'm really not that hungry. I think I'm going to take a shower. But herbal tea would be nice," I reply.

"When did you start drinking herbal tea?" he asks.

"Erick got me into it. It might just be better than coffee when I ain't feeling well."

"Nothing's better than coffee," Davis signs back.

119

"Who's Erick, baby?" Mama asks, fiddling with the oxygen tubes in her nose.

"A friend from school."

"Sure, I tell you that you drink too much coffee, and to try my herbal stuff, but you don't listen to me ..." Mama says with a tired smirk and a roll of her eyes.

"That's not true, Mama."

"Davis, sweetie, can you put this back on the coffee table," Mama asks, handing him the portrait of her and her sister.

"Sure."

***

I am dreaming when the phone wakes me up. Lying on my full size bed, I turn onto my stomach and pull the blanket over my head with a moan. After the fourth ring, I grab the cordless phone lying next to me on the nightstand that Davis and Alex, his older brother, had made for me for Christmas, in Alex's carpentry shop.

"What!?" is my greeting.

"I've been trying to get a hold of you for two days. Are you okay?" It is Erick. Rubbing my eyes, I wonder how rude it would be to simply hang up and go back to sleep.

"What time is it?"

"Eight thirty ... Did I wake you up?"

"Yea ..."

"Sorry."

"No, you aren't."

"Okay, obviously this is a bad time, so how about I call you when you're much more awake and pleasant—"

"Wait—I'm sorry."

"I'm just calling because I am concerned. Where have you been? Why don't you have a cell phone?"

"I've been busy ... I guess I should have called you." *Not that I really thought about you.*

"So, everything's okay? I mean, you weren't at Quikstop yesterday morning, either, and Luke, the guy at the register, said you had some type of emergency and would be out for a few days."

"Everything's okay, dude."

"Good." There is an awkward silence. I'm pretty sure he doesn't believe me.

"I worry about you, you know?" he says to me, finally. I swallow, feeling slightly uncomfortable that he would say something like that. Why would he worry about me? He hardly knows me.

"I thought maybe you told your Mama and she got upset and kicked you out—"

"She doesn't know yet, Erick. Everything's fine, really." I hear Mama coughing in her bedroom. Pushing the mute button on the phone, I yell, "Mama, are you okay? Do you need something to drink?"

"I'm okay."

"Hello, are you still there?" Erick asks.

"Yes. Thanks for calling me. Sorry for worrying you," I say, trying to sound sincere, "Um, so, uh, you wanna get together this weekend? It's my birthday."

"Wait a minute. Are you actually asking me if I want to celebrate your birthday with you?"

"Maybe I am …"

"So, what do you want to do?"

"Hang out with Esperanza and Davis … They're planning a surprise for me but you can come. You can come to my house." I give him directions and Esperanza's number.

"So, are you sure you're okay? Everything's okay?" he repeats. Mama starts coughing again. I want to check on her.

"Things are fine. Call Esperanza and let her know you're coming, okay? I have to do some chores for my mama and get dressed and stuff. I'll call you back later."

"You got my number?"

"On my caller I.D." Mama continues coughing. "Erick, I have to go. Bye."

***

"Happy birthday," Davis greets me as he enters the kitchen. It is seven-thirty, Saturday evening. He puts the two brown grocery bags he is carrying, onto the table.

"What's this?" I sign.

"Your fridge was looking kind of empty the other night, so my Dad and I decided to buy a few things."

"You didn't have to." Shrugging with a grin, "We wanted to," he says.

"How much did you spend?"

"Don't worry about it. Think of it as a birthday gift. Anyway, I think I ate all the leftovers that night, so I should be replacing your food. I eat three times as much as you … How is she? I know Mom is coming by tomorrow so they can talk and watch some new Perry Tyler movie."

"Tyler Perry. You always mess up his name … She is doing better, I guess. She had a headache and had to lay down for a bit. I think I heard her snoring." I tell him how, after I got home from work this afternoon, she and I ate vanilla cake that she had made for me and assured me that my "real" gift was coming; it's just a week late.

"Dad too," Davis says.

"Huh?"

"He's going to give you your gift a little late, too. Dad isn't quite finished putting everything together, yet," he says. For some reason, Mr. Allen has enjoyed giving me elaborate homemade gifts for my birthday, since my fifth birthday. I hardly ever see the guy, since he works like crazy on the farm. However, he always makes it a point to personally give me my gift. When we were younger, Davis used to always whine, "He never does that for any of us."

"Okay, I won't bother her for a hug then. You look great! Did you make the dress?"

I am wearing my white leather strappy high heels and a short cut magenta colored flower print dress. Esperanza had convinced me that it was necessary to dress 'sexy,' tonight.

"Thanks. I made it in December, but it's been too cold to wear … Why don't you have to dress sexy?"

"Girl, I'm always sexy," he signs with a grin.

"Esperanza better be wearing a dress too. I don't want to be the only one that's overdressed."

"Chill. She will. I got you a bottle of Beck's from Alex's stash. It's chilled and ready to go!" He hands me a brown bag for me to look into. There is an orange bow wrapped around the neck of the bottle. My favorite color! I am not supposed to be drinking. Mama has told me that she forbids alcohol in her house. "I don't even care when you're twenty-one or thirty-one years old. There will be no alcohol in my house!" she had yelled to me, after she found I had been drinking at Angela Haussler's party, sophomore year in high school. With those words followed the only time she had ever beaten me. Davis knows this, which is why it's hidden in a bag in case she had been around to see it. I decide to take my chances and drink it because I am pretty sure she probably won't wake up until tomorrow morning.

"Do you know how long I've been waiting to have one of these?"

"I know …" I give him a hug and we both sit down.

"So, are you ready to have a good time?" he asks me.

"I guess. I'm just not sure if I really should go out since Mama is still recovering. I know Mrs. Chapman will be checking in on her, but I still don't know if she'll be okay." Mrs. Chapman is a little old woman across the hall from us that used to babysit me when I was younger.

"And you know your mother will kick your butt if you don't go out and try to have some fun on your birthday. She's expecting you to party hardy and to stay out as long as you can! Kitter's giving you until Thursday off; paid vacation! What more could you possibly ask for?"

"What if Mrs. Chapman—"

"She's a retired nurse, I think she knows how to take care of Mama Sales, Savi."

"Well, you could at least tell me where we're going so she knows where I am—"

"I told Mama Sales the other night. She knows and approves. You worry too much."

"You can never worry too much."

"Drink your beer and relax. If that doesn't work, I've got the other five bottles in the trunk and some freshly rolled joints as a backup plan."

"Trying to turn me into a lush—" A knock at the door interrupts me.

"Come in!" It is Erick and Esperanza.

"¡Feliz cumpleaños!" Esperanza hands me a small gift-wrapped box and gives me a hug. This evening, she smells like lavender with a touch a lemongrass.

"I wouldn't have missed your birthday for the world!" she exclaims. She whirls me around to take a look at my outfit, "Love it. Love it!" I try not to blush.

I am about to give Erick a hug as well when he holds his arms up in the air, steps back, and then asks with suspicion, "You're not actually going to hug me, are you?"

"Of course I am," and I hug him.

"Wow, are you in a good mood or what?"

"Sit down and make yourselves comfortable," I say, as I lead them into the living room. I plop down on my beanbag while they sit on the sofa beside me.

"Want anything to drink?" I ask, swigging back my beer.

"You've turned nineteen, not twenty-one," he says, looking suspiciously at the bottle of beer in my underage hand.

"You're not going to call the cops, are you?" I ask, half-jokingly.

"Nope, just didn't tag you as an underage drinker," he replies.

"Where's your mamá?" Esperanza asks.

"She is napping because she wasn't feeling well, but she made a vanilla cake for me and there's a lot left over if y'all want some."

"You know how she feels about drinking, you rebel," Esperanza says.

"Well, let's get out of here so she doesn't have to know," I say, getting up to grab my coat from the rack near the front door.

"I wanted to say hi to her," Esperanza says with a pout.

"You'll get to, soon," I tell her. She doesn't know about Mama yet.

"Are one of these girls your mother?" Erick asks, grabbing the picture of Mama and Auntie Mama Twin from the coffee table.

"Yup."

"Let me guess ... The one on the right is your Mama," he says.

"Nope. That's my aunt, Mama's fraternal twin sister."

"Oh ... Wow, you look more like your aunt than your Mama."

"I've told her that before," Esperanza says, winking at me.

"When was the picture taken?"

"1985." Erick looks closer at the picture, "Check out the big afros! That's awesome!" I shake my head, rolling my eyes at him.

"What?" he exclaims.

"Sometimes you try too hard," I say.

"What happened here?" Erick asks, gliding his finger over the two-inch long scar in the middle of my forehead.

"She bashed her head on the edge of the coffee table on her fourth birthday. She and I were running around the living room and she tripped," Davis replies.

"I don't remember anything, but I was told that I had twelve stitches, was unconscious for a few days, and had some weird amnesia thing for a year. I actually don't remember anything from after that until the following year, in May. It's really weird." Erick crumples his eyebrows in disbelief, "Are you serious?" Curiously, his fingers find his way to his own scar on his neck, caresses it gently, and then glides his hand down into his pants pocket. I cock my head to the side, wondering if I should inquire about it.

"Yea. I have pictures of me doing stuff: first day of nursery school; pictures from when I went camping in Maine for three weeks with the Allens that following August," I sign and say.

"Let's not talk about this anymore," Davis says. He always becomes weird whenever anyone mentions my scar. I always wonder if he feels bad that he was running after me when I fell.

"Okay, let's take la princesa to the ball!" Esperanza exclaims.

"Get your party on, yo!" Erick continues. I shake my head and roll my eyes, "What the hell was that?"

"Savi, Erick is exempt from his 'lesson' tonight," Esperanza says. Instead of 'getting into it,' I nod and let his silly statement melt away, "Okay then, lessons resume tomorrow. Now, where's my stretch Hummer limo?"

***

"Are you buzzed or drunk?" Erick asks me, two hours later.

"Are you drunk?" Erick repeats. He sounds really far away even though he is sitting right next to me.

"I'm fine," I finally reply. It is amazing how far a fake I.D. can take you. We're in East Hartford, at Salsa Caliente, a nightclub and restaurant with live Latin music performances. Tonight, Roja, one of my favorite groups, is performing. Compared to the picture of her on my CD cover, Tina Santiago, the lead singer, is ten times sexier in person. *Jesus, that succulent mouth and the sounds that emanate from it.* I smirk to myself in drunken ecstasy, wondering what notes I could make her trill if we were spread out on a bed somewhere.

"So wonderful that you're enjoying this!" Esperanza exclaims to me. With an enthusiastic nod, I giggle, "I can't remember the last time I had this much fun—" and interrupt myself with a hiccup.

"You've had two beers, two shots of Jose Cuervo, and a Margarita; you're wasted," Erick tells me. He signs to Davis that I am drunk. Sitting across from me, Davis says, "I thought so. She's been smiling too much to be sober. Savi, you're too tiny to handle all this stuff. No more Guinness for you!"

"You guys act like I never smile," I sign and say.

"Well, can you remember the last time you smiled?" Davis asks. Stealing a French fry from off of his plate I say, "Shut up," followed by a sly smirk. Roja starts playing a salsa.

"Oh, I love this song. This is the song Esperanza and I used to salsa to!" I exclaim.

"Let's go up and dance!" Esperanza tells me. Growing up, she and I would turn up the stereo and dance to Roja in her living room, along with her sisters.

"Come on, girl! Let's tear up the dance floor," Esperanza exclaims, grabbing my hand and pulling me up from my seat. Dressed in a flowing satin black dress and red pumps, how could I say no?

"They're really good dancers," I hear Davis tell Erick as I leave the table. I definitely feel the effects of the mélange of alcohol in my system as I walk to the dance floor. Maintaining coordination in four-inch heels would be a fun little feat.

She twirls me around, then says, "Let's do our thang from last summer! Do you remember it?" Giggling from obvious inebriation, I nod, "Let's go for it!"

"Move them hips, sexy Mama!" Esperanza exclaims to me. Within thirty-seconds of starting our salsa routine, the people on the dance floor have made a circle around Esperanza and me. They are whistling and clapping to the beat of the song. I see that Erick and Davis have joined the circle as well. I haven't felt so free all year. Why can't this last forever?

As we're face to face, she mouths to me, "Sexy Savannah!" and then gives me that cute little mischievous signature grin of hers.

You're so beautiful ... God, you're so beautiful. She still smells like lemongrass and lavender. I edit my current fantasy by envisioning myself being naked with Esperanza, somewhere on a luscious green meadow, sprawled out on top of a soft cotton blanket; Tina Santiago singing to us while Esperanza and I make love.

Several minutes later, the song ends. We receive enthusiastic applause and whistles. She and I are still face-to-face. *Honey. Sweet honey. Her lips, so luscious and enticing. Do they too taste like sweet honey?* My heart is beating quickly as I stare into the eyes of the love of my life. She puts her hands around my shoulders, pulling me closer to give me a hug. I feel I can do anything right now. And what I really want to do is put my arms around her and kiss her, gently ... gently ... gently ...

***

"... Savannah?" My eyes are closed. Am I lying on my back? Why am I laying on my back and who is calling my name?

"Savannah?" Someone pinches my cheek and I finally open my eyes. It is Mr. Erick Roberts. Why don't I hear any more music?

"How's my favorite lush?" he greets me. Sitting up quickly, I ask, "Where'd everybody go?"

"Wow, you were really wasted last night."

"Last night!?" I finally realize that I am not at Salsa Caliente but in what appears to be a bedroom.

"You're at my place in Glastonbury. It's ten-thirty Sunday morning." Blinking several times, I am still very confused and repeat, "I don't understand. What happened? Where are Davis and Esperanza?"

"Damn Savannah, what's the last thing you remember?"

"What happened!?"

"Calm down! You got cocked off your ass, that's what … What's the last thing you remember?" My mind races, but several seconds later, I reply, "Dancing a salsa with Esperanza, of course."

"And …?" Crumpling my eyebrows, "And what?"

"And you've conveniently forgotten the scandalous part?" My eyebrows rise in inquiry. Erick continues, "Why, you and I both concluded that heterosexuality is the way to go … and we made hot passionate love all night."

"You lying bastard!" And I try to punch him in the shoulder. Missing by a long shot, he starts laughing, "Damn, are you still drunk?" I aim for his shoulder, hitting it this time. My head starts spinning as the most sickening feeling enters my stomach. Lying back down, moaning, I say, "Jesus, I feel like I'm going to die."

"You're not dying. You're hungover … Just don't puke again. These are Ralph Lauren Polo bedspreads."

"I'm not going to puke on your precious elitist sheets."

"Wow, you told me that about my car last night, too." Closing my eyes in embarrassment, "I did not puke in your car, did I?"

"Okay, you didn't. You puked just before we got you into the car."

"I was not that drunk. What the hell really happened, Erick? Stop joking around, please."

"You stop. Are you serious that the last thing you remember is dancing with Esperanza?"

"Yes, goddammit!" I nearly scream, opening my eyes.

"Jeez, calm down. I believe you." He stands up, puts his hands in his pockets, and then slowly begins to pace back and forth.

"Stop that! You're making me nervous," I tell him.

"I'm making you nervous? I don't even know if I should tell you since you're in such a bad mood—And after I opened my home to you!"

"Goddammit, Erick—"

"Okay, you asked for it," he takes a deep breath, "For starters, after last night, Esperanza has most likely concluded that you want to get your groove on with the women ..." Don't panic yet. Davis already knew, right? However, my heart is already beating one million miles per hour as I wait for him to tell me the worse.

"So, what did I do?" I ask through gritted teeth.

"Well, in the middle of the dance floor, she gave you a hug and was about to kiss you on the cheek. You wrapped your arms around her neck and kissed her right on the lips. You wouldn't let go for about ten, maybe fifteen-seconds. I'm not talking about a little peck, either." I put the pillow over my face and groan. Maybe this is a dream. What else can it be? When I take the pillow away from my face, I will be laying in my bedroom. However, as I remove the pillow, I see that it is still Erick's bedroom.

"Do you want me to continue?" Reluctantly, I nod.

"Well, she was totally cool with it—I mean, she didn't freak out too much. Initially, I think it confused and caught her off guard—"

"The whole restaurant saw. I'll never be able to go there again."

"Stop overreacting. Honestly, no one cares. You know that kind of stuff turns straight men on. I mean, most of them were cheering you on. Anyhoo, to make a long story short, you're now out to your closest friends, and guess what? They don't hate you. Therefore, there's nothing to really be depressed about. So, get up, freshen up, and let's start this glorious Sunday!"

"So, that's it? That's the whole story? I thought you said the night was scandalous. It's much worse and you just don't want to tell me because you don't think I can handle it. You're lying." Erick shakes his head and points his finger at me, "You know, sometimes I think you like being miserable."

"Yea, well—Well, sometimes I think—well, you're … um …" He raises his eyebrows, awaiting my rebuttal. However, nothing witty enters my hung over mind right now, just the desire to vomit and maybe pass out again.

"You can save the insult for when you're coherent. You want some water? Something to eat? I think Davis and Esperanza are attempting to make vegan waffles—"

"Esperanza's here!?"

"Where else would she be?" I pull the sheets over my head, "Why the hell—What the hell? I am so confused."

"It started snowing pretty badly last night. We thought it would be stupid to drive any further than necessary. After passing by several car accidents and not being able to see clearly, we decided that it would be best to stay at my place until the storm passed. Plus, Davis wasn't sure if you should go back to your home if you're trashed. You're mother would—"

"Oh no! Mama!" The covers fly off my head and I jump out of bed. Ugh, too fast. Ugh, my head. I try to not vomit and lose my balance from dizziness and dehydration. Erick reaches out to catch me before I take a nosedive into the smooth cherry hardwood floor.

"Whoa sailor, not so fast," he commands, his arms around my waist, "Esperanza called your mother about an hour ago. Everything's cool," he assures me.

"You don't understand, I have to get home—where are my clothes? Let go!" He continues to hold me by the waist, but loosens his grip, "I just don't want you to fall … Davis says that your mother says not to worry about getting home in a hurry because it's too dangerous to drive. She says Mrs. Chaplain—"

"Mrs. Chapman." He let's go of my waist, "Thank you!" I shout with annoyance.

"Whatever … Mrs. Chapman is keeping her company. Anyway, it's still snowing." I wonder if Davis has told Erick about Mama. I hope not. It's none of his damn business.

"I do not like being miserable," I exclaim defensively, sitting back down on the bed. Shaking my head, I cannot believe what I did last night—and remembering nothing! The only time I get to experience Esperanza's lips on mine, and I can't even remember what it felt like! I start laughing to myself. Why is this a surprise? Of course I'd have to forget the very moment I had always desired. Of course!

"Hello? What are you laughing at?" Erick asks, sitting down next to me.

"My life, of course!" There is a knock at the door.

"Who is it?" Erick asks.

"Esperanza ... Is she okay? Can I come in?" Quickly, I cover Erick's mouth and whisper, "Tell her I'm still sleeping." He pulls my hand away from his mouth, "After your grumpy attitude, why should I?" I push him away, lie back in bed, and then pull the covers over my head.

"You aren't going to hide in here forever," he whispers to me. He finally responds to Esperanza, "She's awake. Come on in."

I cannot believe he just said that. I'm never talking to him again. This isn't a joke ...

Breathing slowly, my ears tune in on the click of the bedroom door.

"She's hiding," Erick tells Esperanza. Several seconds later, someone is tugging at the covers. It is probably her.

I can't look her in the eyes. There's no shame in that, right?

"I'm going to eat breakfast. This is a hopeless effort," I hear Erick say. No, please don't leave me alone with her.

"Savi, you have to come out of there sometime," Esperanza whispers.

"I was drunk!" I exclaim without thinking. That was brilliant. Simply brilliant, you moron.

Tugging again at the covers, she says, "You're not going to talk to me through these blankets." Slowly, I reveal my face to her. She is wearing a Harvard University gray tee shirt and matching crimson sweat pants. She looks great in anything, I think.

"Well, now you are no longer drunk," she says with a smile.

"For the record, the last thing I remember is doing the salsa." One eyebrow raised, she replies unconvincingly, "Really?"

"I swear ..."

"So, why were you covering your head with the blanket?" I look away from her face, shrug, then repeat, "I was drunk … Erick kind of—well … um, told me what he thinks he saw—or rather, happened … I was drunk," … and horny … and drunk.

"Stop lying and tell your best friend what's up?"

"I was drunk. People do strange things when they're drunk."

"In wine there is truth, girl."

"And it was beer and hard liquor, not wine. There's no truth in beer." She sighs, "You know, I'm not disgusted if that's what you're thinking. Yeah, I was a little freaked out when you lip-locked me. At first I thought you were just really drunk, but then you started saying a lot of things to me once we got you into the car." Groaning, I wonder how she can expect me to look her in the eyes as she is telling me this?

"Savi, there's nothing to be ashamed about. Nothing's changed between us." Closing my eyes, I try to convince myself that she is right; that I should not be ashamed of the desires I have. However, it does not work. Instead, I feel as if I should be ashamed; ashamed because it doesn't seem right to feel any other way.

"Savannah, my cousin Lucinda, in Toronto, is a lesbian."

"Why are you telling me this?" is my reply.

"Because you're a les—"

"Please don't say that. I am not. I was drunk, Esperanza." *Jesus, why can't I think of another line?*

"Stop being silly. You're the only one making a huge deal out of this. Notice that Erick, Davis, and I didn't leave you behind at the restaurant last night? We're still here, as your friends. We even made you some waffles! Bottom line: we don't care that you like girls, so stop pretending that you're not attracted to them, or that last night was some type of alcohol-induced 'never again.' Now, get out of bed and eat some waffles with us!"

My response to her is a blank stare. Throwing her arms up in the air, she exclaims, "Dios mio, are you even listening to me? Answer me, dammit! I want to go and eat some waffles!"

***

Sitting at Erick's kitchen table, I stare at my Belgian waffle wondering where my dress is; wondering whether I puked on it; wondering if, after talking to Mama on the phone, she really doesn't need me back anytime soon. "Enjoy your free time, baby. Don't you worry about me," she had told me. Enjoy my free time? I have begun to suspect that I do not know how to enjoy free time. Had Erick been right? Do I really like to be miserable? *Oh, what does he know? Nothing, because he's never ever been poor. Why would anyone enjoy being miserable—*

"Savannah, you've been staring at that waffle for the last five minutes," Davis says to me. Without looking up, I shrug in reply. Lifting up my fork, I poke at it several times, sniff, and then put my fork back down. I don't enjoy being miserable. I slouch down into the brushed stainless steel dining chair. *Who buys stainless steel chairs for a dining table anyway?* My toes grace the warm hard wood flooring of the dining room. On the left of me is the entrance to Erick's kitchen. Ceiling tract lights brightly illuminate a newly renovated kitchen that is filled with high-end culinary purchases like a *Vita-Mix* blender and *Le Creuset* cookware and bakeware. On the side of his enormous stainless steel refrigerator is a bookcase filled with vegetarian and vegan cookbooks. On top of the bookcase are photos of some way too happy and smiling blonde chick—probably his little sister—hanging on the ivory painted wall.

"I don't enjoy being miserable, jerk," I mumble, spontaneously grabbing one of my two knives on the side of my plate, and then stab my waffle. All around my plate are too many utensils with various functions that I could care less about. They're all supposed to be for my brunch. *Why do I need two different spoons anyway? What's the point of a small and big fork? A red cloth napkin? Why?*

"Are you still drunk?" Erick asks me. Taking the knife out of the waffle, I look up and point it at him, "I don't enjoy being miserable."

"What is she talking about?" Esperanza asks.

"Who said anything about that?" Erick asks.

"What did she say?" Davis signs to Erick.

"She doesn't enjoy being miserable," he signs back.

"Well, I don't enjoy being miserable," I sign and say.

"Who said you did?" Davis replies.

"That reject sitting over there," I say, pointing to Erick.

"Hey, this reject let you sleep in his bed, while he slept on the floor."

"I mean, you hardly even know me. How can you make such an accusation?" I continue. Taking a sip from his orange juice, Erick replies, "It wasn't an accusation. I was merely speculating. You were beginning to get on my nerves. Sorry if I hurt your feelings, but it was just something I had to say."

"You didn't hurt my feelings. You just made me mad." My cheeks quiver a bit, but then I quickly command myself not to cry. I rub my cheeks furiously.

"I always make you mad, Savannah. I thought you knew that by now," he says with a smirk, "Now put the butter knife down before you hurt yourself."

"Can I have your waffle if you're not going to eat it?" Davis asks me.

"There's plenty of *vegan* ones left if you want some," Esperanza says, pointing to a plate of waffles with interesting texture and consistency. She intentionally emphasizes vegan. I pretend not to notice.

"Um, how about I leave those all for you guys?" Davis asks, not taking his eyes away from my waffle. Shrugging, I answer, "Go for it." He beams with joy, and then pierces my waffle with his matte silver fork.

"We should play in the snow after," Erick signs and says.

"That sounds like fun," Davis replies, a mouthful of waffle in his pie-hole.

"Can't you eat with your mouth closed without talking, you pig," I sign and say to Davis. Esperanza shakes her head and then shakes her right index finger at me, "You know, it's not nice to insult a human being by calling them a pig. And pigs go through so much suffering just so you can get your breakfast bacon sandwich from McDonalds and then die from a heart attack—"

"Ugh, not now Esperanza. Seriously, I just can't listen to that right now," I fume. Esperanza shakes her and then whispers to herself, barely loud enough for me to hear, "If not *now*, then when?" She then gives a glance to Erick, gesturing with her raised eyebrows that she is looking for his support. He returns her glance with raised eyebrows as well, and then shrugs his shoulders, "Yea, probably not the best time, but I know what you mean."

"You know, just because you have a million annoying vegetarian and vegan cookbooks in your kitchen and wear that stupid PETA button all the time, doesn't make you some perfectly enlightened human being. A gazillion vegetarian books but I bet you don't own even one book about racism or white privilege," I say to Erick, as well as sign to Davis. My head begins to throb again. *Ugh, why are we even having this stupid conversation about pigs?*

"I don't really care to get into this … Anyway, Savi is just being Savi," Davis says and signs nonchalantly.

"Whatever, another time then," Erick repeats with a sigh. Esperanza crumples her eyebrows at me with disappointment. Well, what does she expect? I'm hung over and cranky and she knows not to talk smack about my McDonalds.

"*Whatever* … Can we just go back to East Lebanon, since it stopped snowing?" I ask.

"Cold weather's good for hangovers," Esperanza tells me.

"I'm not hung over and I don't feel like being wet and cold."

"Come on. Stop being miserable and start having fun," Erick tells me.

"If you say that one more time, I am going to stab you with this overpriced knife."

"I got it at Williams and Sonoma and it wasn't overpriced. You know, I just don't understand why you can't tell us why you're always pissed off. Do you always have to resort to aggression and violence? Let's talk about it," Erick says, pouring some rice milk into his cup.

"He's got a good point," Esperanza says, putting her arm around my shoulder.

"Do you want to talk about what happened last night or something?" Erick asks. Rolling my eyes and sighing, "No! Can I just go home after breakfast?"

"I really think you need to talk about last night so you can see that it wasn't a big deal. You don't need to make a big deal out of it. Believe me, there will be many more embarrassing moments in your lesbian future in comparison to last night," Erick assures. Before Davis can request a translation, Erick signs it.

"Anyway, Esperanza says you're a great kisser!" Davis adds, puckering up his lips, pretending that he is kissing someone. Esperanza giggles then nods in agreement. I look down at my plate, surprising myself by smiling a bit. I try not to let them see it, but it's too late.

"Ha, we made her smile!" Erick exclaims, his blue eyes sparkling with fulfillment, "My work here on planet Earth is done."

"No you didn't," I say, forcing the smile to leave my usually sullen face.

"Eat something. You're losing your curvaceous booty. You know we can't have you losing that," Esperanza says. She puts some home fries onto my plate, takes a vegan waffle from off of the teal colored serving plate, then lays it on top of the home fries. She continues to chomp on the tofu scramble Erick had made for her.

"You know you love us," Erick says, then pours some apple juice into my cobalt blue tumbler, "Drink up so you don't get dehydrated, okay?" I playfully flick him on the forehead.

"Ow." Before he can ask 'why,' Davis translates, "It's her way of saying, 'Thank you.'"

Shaking his head, Erick replies, "I guess I'll take whatever I can get."

***

I don't talk to anyone about anything. Even though everyone else had wanted to enjoy being wet and cold in the snow, Erick has decided to simply take me back home; then, they will play on the East Lebanon town green. My persistent whining has won.

Driving home, I remain quiet in the back seat with Esperanza beside me. I wish Davis had chosen to sit next to me, but he claims that he is too tall to sit in the back, comfortably.

"Enjoy your free time," Mama's voice resonates in the back of my mind. I don't know how to, I admit. Have I gotten so used to living in misery? It's not true. I don't enjoy it. I know I don't enjoy it ...

"Hey, can I meet your mother?" Erick asks, as we pull into my apartment's parking lot, thirty minutes later.

"Hey, I haven't said hello to your mother yet, either," Esperanza says.

"If you really want to," I answer, slowly opening the car door and stepping onto the snow. As I approach our door, I wonder if it really is a good idea for them to see her. What if she is sitting on the sofa with her oxygen in her nose? What will I say? What will she say? What will they say?

Davis puts his arm around my shoulders, and as if reading my mind, whispers, "Don't worry, there's nothing to worry about."

"So, I finally get to meet the woman who gave you life," Erick says as I grab our front door handle. Spontaneously, I turn around to face Erick and Esperanza. I don't know what comes over me, but before I can think through it logically, I blurt out, "She's not well."

"We know. She fell down the stairs. We know," Esperanza says. Bowing my head, and with a whisper, I return, "No, I mean, she's really sick. She has late stage emphysema. It's ... killing her." I feel my eyes water with tears and a knot forming in my throat. Davis pulls me close to him and gives me a much-needed hug. We all slip into an awkward silence for a good ten-seconds. I feel Erick put his hand on my back, caressing it, "I didn't know." Davis carefully lets go of me and then I slowly turn around. I look at the floor, now having second thoughts about letting them into my secret war trenches.

Esperanza wraps her long arms around me and whispers, "Look up at me." Reluctantly, I reveal my face to her. A tear finally trickles down my cheek. Esperanza's finger gently wipes away my quiet and private suffering.

"No more secrets, okay?" she whispers. The insistence in her eyes is penetrating. I feel it pierce the center of my heart and bounce off the edge of my fading soul. From some unforeseen light in the dismal hall, her eyes glisten with a strong sense of hope. With a deep sigh and slight nod of my head, I give her a tiny smile of assurance. She kisses me on the cheek, then whispers, "Come on. Let's give Mama Sales a big hug."

CHAPTER THIRTEEN

I admit it.

I vowed to never go to Greenwich Village with Erick. Less than a week ago, I thought it had been a stupid and dangerous idea. A week later, I am exiting the Amtrak train at New York Port Authority; the round trip ticket, a birthday gift from Davis, Erick, and Esperanza.

"This is the hugest bus and train station!"

"See how small you've been thinking? 'Hugest' isn't a word," Erick tells me. I roll my eyes, but then give him a smirk so he knows I'm trying not to become angry over every little thing he says.

It is Monday morning, less than two days after my embarrassing birthday. Several hours after Erick had dropped me off at home, Esperanza had called me.

"Girl, we're picking you up tomorrow at seven in the morning."

"Esperanza, what are you talking about?"

"Erick and I are taking you to New York. To The Village. It's on us, so don't say you're too broke to go."

"That's not a good idea—"

"No, Savi, it isn't an option. You are going and that's final. We are officially interfering with the way you view life … Be ready tomorrow and bring a huge smile on your face!"

"But—"

"Good. See you then." I remember staring at the phone receiver for a few minutes, dumbfounded, battling with whether I should call her back. However, I had surprised myself by not calling back to argue.

…So, here we are: Esperanza, Erick, and I. I am disappointed that Davis is not here. He couldn't get out of work. He had given me his digital camera to photo-document everything, though. I turn the camera on to take a picture of the train.

"There are so many people," I tell them, picking up my bright orange duffel bag from off of the ground.

139

"This is nothing. Wait until we get out onto the street," Davis tells me. Then, scrutinizing my bag, he says, "Well, at least we'll find you if you get lost in a crowd."

"Shut up. Bright orange is my favorite color."

"It is kind of ghetto," Esperanza says with a giggle. Erick continues with, "Well, I didn't really think it was my place to say anything."

"Paaaleease. Like either of you have ever been to the ghetto," I say, trying not to become annoyed that everyone seems to use that term so sparingly these days.

"Big Apple, here we come!" Esperanza explains, buttoning up her wool coat and wrapping her scarf around her neck. I shake my head and tug at her scarf. She never got used to the cold northeast, despite having been away from Guatemala for ten years. It is nearly sixty degrees today. Erick and I are wearing light jackets. It is hard to believe we had snow the day before.

"It's not that cold," Erick tells her, tugging at her coat, playfully. Clutching my bag tightly, I stand frozen at my spot, not really sure what we will be doing next. A Black man with long neatly manicured dreadlocks passes by me, nods, and then says, "Hey sistah. Lookin' ruff 'n tuff wit cha afro puff," and continues walking by. After several seconds, he turns his head around, smiles back at me, and then continues walking toward the exit.

"Isn't that cute?" Esperanza says.

"What?" I ask, clutching my bag tighter, feeling very awkward, wondering about my ginormous breasts, as usual, while simultaneously wondering if I really should have worn the puff and left my electric hot comb at home.

"Savannah just got hit on," she tells Erick.

"I did?"

"Sure you did. He was hitting on you."

"No he wasn't," I refute.

"You're a very attractive girl with the most beautiful lips I've ever seen. Why wouldn't you turn a few heads?" Erick says. Rolling my eyes, I start to say something when Esperanza covers my mouth, "He just complimented you. You say, 'Why thank you Mr. Roberts.

You're not so bad looking yourself.'" Uncovering my mouth, she says, "Well?"

"Thanks, Erick. That was very kind of you," is my reluctant reply, sprinkled with a touch of sincerity.

"Wow, Savannah," he begins, pauses for a second, then continues, "That almost sounded sincere." Smirking, I then look to my right; a colorful advertisement for Abacavir, pasted beside me, catches my attention. Cocking my head to the side, I wonder why the ad tells me, "Ask your doctor about Abacavir."

"It's a drug for people living with HIV," Erick tells me.

"Oh," is my response, looking back at she and Erick.

"Let's go, y'all. This place is crazy and this chica is hungry!" Esperanza exclaims.

"Food it is!" Erick exclaims, putting his arms around both our shoulders and leading the way.

***

"I don't understand," I say, looking into the store's window. Ninety minutes later, after having eaten, we are on our way to Erick's ex-boyfriend's place. Erick and Esperanza have decided to stop and look into a store called Candyland.

"You know, fun tasty stuff," Erick explains with a grin. Peering into the window, I reply, "But I don't see any candy." Esperanza starts laughing. Erick turns to her, "Is she for real? She really doesn't know what this store sells?" Erick steps back, then takes a picture of the storefront with his Blackberry cell phone.

"Don't talk about me like I'm not here!" I exclaim, still trying to figure out where all the candy is. My stomach is craving dark chocolate. I see Erick's reflection in the window. He is trying to suppress a smile for some reason.

"Savi, you know, tasty treats? Vibrators, blowup dolls—"

"Gross!" I exclaim, cutting Erick off, then turning around to cover my eyes.

"Now now, let's be open-minded," he tells me, trying to take my hand away from my face.

"Let's go before someone sees us here," I say.

"I wanna go in," Erick and Esperanza demand at the same time.

"Well, I'm not going in there." Disgusting.

"What happened to changing our perspective on life?" Esperanza asks, trying to pull me along to follow Erick. I won't budge and exclaim, "No!" I wonder if they can tell that I am blushing with embarrassment.

"No one in the store or out of the store is going to care that you are looking at dildos and anal beads. You should know what's out there and then decide if you like it or not, ya know?" Erick explains. Esperanza nods, "Come on, it'll be fun!"

Dildos! Oh my god! And what on God's Earth is an anal bead!? I give Erick a look of horror and he cracks up, "Can I take a picture of your face at this very moment in time? Priceless!" Before I can say 'no,' he has taken the picture. I growl at him and he simply shakes his head in amusement. He turns the Blackberry around to view the picture of me, Esperanza peaking over his shoulder.

"Kodak moment," she says.

"I just emailed it to your school account, Savi," he says to me, clicking away at his annoying little overpriced gadget.

Several minutes later, I am sitting in the corner of the shop, trying to ignore the fact that I am in such a sinful space. We are the only customers there. On one side of me is a display of vibrators; on the other side are black leather spiked neck collars. In the middle of the store, Erick is on all fours, making howling noises as Esperanza sits on his back, hitting him on the butt with a short rubber whip. The man behind the cash register is laughing uncontrollably. I can't help but to grin myself. Esperanza turns to me, and then smiles, "You want some too?" I don't know whether to be disgusted, intrigued, or amused. Silently, I shake my head, slowly feeling my underwear become wet as she bounces on top of him. *Why does she do this to me? Am I straight if a girl bouncing on top of a guy—a gay guy—turns me on?*

"I think we're traumatizing her," Erick says, Esperanza getting off his back, thirty-seconds later. *Maybe I'm bisexual?*

"Or turning her on," Esperanza says with a 'dirty girl' giggle.

"So, what are you two looking for?" The dude behind the register asks them.

"Longer orgasms with vegan lubricants!" Esperanza exclaims. I cannot believe she has just said that. *Vegan lubricant?*

"Maybe a cock ring. I can't find my old one," Erick follows. I cannot believe how strange she and Erick have been acting, ever since we've stepped into the city. What is wrong with you two?

"And what about your friend in the corner over there?" he asks, leaning over the counter to get a better view of me. I try not to make eye contact with him, but do anyway. He's hard to look at because he isn't wearing a shirt, both his nipples pierced. He's a Black man of about forty years.

"I'm fine, thank you, sir," I say very rapidly to him, trying to smile but probably looking more like a deer caught in headlights.

"Actually, what do you have for a repressed newly out prudish lesbian who can't admit she's horny? She just came out a week ago and her favorite color is bright tacky orange," Erick says. I remain in the chair, biting down hard on my bottom lip. Once again, my heart begins to beat quickly at the sound of the l-word.

"Hey kid, I've got something special for new family members," the clerk says to me. I remain frozen in the chair, not quite sure what family I have joined.

"She's never been to The Village—or NYC for that matter. Comes from a place where there are more chickens than people," Erick explains.

"Come on Savannah, stop being a dork," Esperanza says, walking towards me, rubber whip still in her left hand. She grabs my hand and then pulls me up. Several seconds later, I am standing in front of the clerk. He has a big and kind smile on his face, making the butterflies in my stomach slowly drop dead.

"So, you're a rookie at this, eh? Well, welcome to the family," he says in a congratulatory tone. He extends his hand out to me and I shake it, "Daniel Jackson. Out since 1995. I opened the store the same year."

"Savannah Penelope Sales. Kind of out since last week," I let go of his hand, and wonder what else I should do. Am I really 'out?'

"So, how long are you staying here?"

143

"Tomorrow we leave. We just got in today," I whisper.

"It's Monday night, but some lesbian clubs might be open. Crazy Nanny's perhaps ... but y'all look a little young for clubs—you are over eighteen, right? This little one looks like she's about twelve," he says, pointing to me. He continues, "Or is it because Black don't crack?"

I smirk since Mama used to always say the same thing. We promptly show him our I.D.s to put his mind at ease that we're not too young to be in a sex toy store. After, he reaches underneath the counter to get something. Several seconds later, he hands me a small gift box, "Here. It's on the house. For making it through your first week. I know it's hard at first, but it does get better." Opening the box, I see a thin silver chain necklace with small metallic rainbow rings.

"Wow. Thank you very much," I reply with genuine sincerity. Kindness from strangers isn't something I run into too often.

"Thank you for coming out. There's strength in numbers and only death in silence, baby girl. Strength in numbers!"

CHAPTER FOURTEEN

I was more comfortable in the porn shop, I think, biting my lower lip nervously. My neurotic anxiety continues as I wonder if my duffel bag really does look "ghetto," now that it has migrated from the top of an Amtrak luggage compartment to the stately and "classy" floor of the most excessively glamorous and expensive home I have ever been allowed to enter.

"One person lives here?" I had exclaimed twenty minutes earlier, as Erick led Esperanza and I to what I can only describe as an estate that has historically probably only welcomed Black and brown folk onto its property, as long as they were wearing a butler or maid's uniform—hell, maybe even shackles on their ankles.

When Erick had rung the doorbell, encircled by an ornately golden fixture, I had expected a prissy clone to answer the door. However, there had been no "mammy" servant to greet us. My pessimistic expectation had been replaced by a tall lanky twenty-something year old white boy with curly black hair, green eyes, a sunburst tattoo on his right forearm, and one of the warmest smiles I have ever received from any white boy.

Sitting in the living room, I am too scared to even touch anything. The living room is easily as big—if not bigger—than my entire apartment. I am feeling intimidated and uncomfortable. This is absolutely ridiculous that some people are allowed to live this way.

"… and the renovations look great," Erick continues, commenting on this ostentatious abode. Esperanza is sitting next to me on a sofa that I have just learned is a "one of a kind," shipped directly from a nineteenth century Japanese-style furniture artisan the other week. Who knew that nineteenth century Japanese-style furniture artisans even existed? Of course if I were to pose that question to Erick, he'd probably cheerfully say, "Everyone knows that."

"How old were we the last time we were here? It looked completely different. Kind of drab. Must've cost him at least a few million." 'Him' being Troy's uncle.

"Three million, actually," Troy corrects Erick.

"Damn!" Esperanza and I say in unison. *Gee, is anyone else here uncomfortable talking about excessiveness so nonchalantly?* I then think of all the amazing medical care Mama could get with such money, but then try to tell myself not to be jealous or to hate this Troy fellow and his uncle who owns the home. After all, I do know nothing about them. The new Savannah isn't supposed to make snap judgments about rich white people.

"Well, Uncle Stewart needed to jet to Italy for a few months. He told me to stay here and babysit the place for about ten months—maybe even longer if he finds more opportunity in Florence. I mean, he's got a house there, but he really doesn't want to get rid of this place just yet, because of how much money he put into restoring it." Gag, gag, gag. I'm about to say something when Esperanza reads my mind, covertly nudging me in the side with her elbow to keep my mouth shut ... unless I can say whatever I want to say in a not-so-angry-Savannah manner.

"Lucky bastard! How are classes?" Erick asks.

"Ahhh. Don't remind me," Troy says, rolling his eyes, sighing and throwing back his head dramatically.

"What happened?" Erick asks.

"I kind of bombed my linguistics final."

"That's a first," Erick notes.

"Well, I had to spend most of finals week with Andre. Although I did study for it, I pulled an all-nighter staying up with him at the hospital, and on top of stress, distress, and lack of sleep, I was brain dead. Damn, when I got the final back, I saw that I hadn't even written my name down correctly. The prof should have given me an F, but I told her what was up and she let me retake it."

"He's better now, right? I thought he and Keller went up to Canada for a ski vacation in January," Erick asks. I start fidgeting, feeling isolated from the conversation. Even though the new Savannah isn't supposed to be judgmental, I think, *this is absolutely ridiculous and insulting. Why are they talking as if we're not here? Why'd I come to New York? I should be home with Mama.*

"Yea. He's on a new prescription and Lisa is making him exercise with her everyday to build up his respiratory system and cardio and stuff. I'm doing weight training with him three times a week and Stephanie is bringing him to a raw foods nutritionist."

"How is that crazy girl?"

"She finally started talking to me again. We're on good terms. I think we just needed to talk and straighten some things out. We're cool now, I guess. She broke up with Kara, finally. I guess she's admitting to herself that I was right about that whacked out dyke and that she was only holding her back."

"So, things are good?"

"Yep ... You look good."

"You do too."

"So, where'd you grow up? You have an accent," I finally ask, trying to get into the conversation. However, I sincerely can't say that I care where this man or is uncle are from.

"Johannesburg in South Africa." Sarcastically I think, *Of course the first person I ever meet from Africa is a white man. Explains how your family acquired so much 'honest' wealth—okay, no snap judgments, Savannah!*

"Oh, that's interesting. Did your family have to jet to the states after Mandela was freed?" Esperanza asks him. I try not to smirk at the candor and bluntness of her statement. He shakes his head slowly, "No, we moved to Weston before all that stuff happened. My dad and uncle became increasingly outspoken about their beliefs in advocating for an anti-apartheid state. That didn't really fly in their companies, so we moved to Weston. He and my uncle started their own investment-banking firm in 1987 ... I know what you're thinking, Ms. Esperanza ..." he begins, peering at her with his warm eyes, "Well, none of their investments were in South Africa, so my uncle's estate is conscience-free."

"Well, such accoutrements of wealth can't be completely conscience-free, but I do give him an A for effort," Esperanza says with a tone of eloquent sincerity and equally warm eyes. She wraps her left arm around me, "So, where are Savi and I sleeping?"

"On the third floor. I burned lavender and jasmine incense in there for you two, and you have your own bathroom."

"I love jasmine!" Esperanza exclaims.

"I know, Erick told me." Though she is holding me close to the warmness of her body, I still continue to feel very cold and isolated from the conversation and environment. I am in awe of how seamlessly Esperanza handles these situations, simultaneously infusing assertiveness with sincere love towards these folk.

"How's my gal? You hungry or tired or something? You're kind of quiet," my optimistic female counterpart asks me.

"I'm okay," I lie with a murmur. However, my heart and blood boil noisily from within, wanting to convert my suppressed silence into outwardly aggression and howl at Erick about the audacity of bringing me here, especially after seeing where Mama and I live.

"We'll be eating soon. My friend Chinua is going to join us if that's okay. Erick, this is the guy I was telling you about. Wait until you see him. He's gorgeous."

Shaking his head, Erick tells us, "Troy is in love with this straight guy who's engaged and is in his statistics class. His fiancée is in California, finishing up her doctoral work, so Troy is going to make his move. He is convinced that he can make him fall in love with him—"

"I never said that—and I'm not making any move on him! I was joking," he exclaims innocently. Turning to Esperanza and I, Troy continues, "We're going to see Chinua's best friend perform at the restaurant we're heading to in a bit. His name is Cesar and he impersonates James Brown and other singers. He's really cool. He's an amazing man. Has done a lot for transgender rights and awareness. He led the trans pride parade, last summer, and started that petition against Delmore College, in Manhattan, because they denied tenure to a transgender professor. The college reversed their decision last month."

"Sounds like my kind of guy. Not scared to fight for what's right," Esperanza says.

What's transgender? Is that like transvestite? Should I ask? Maybe they'll just think I'm stupid. I then start becoming worried about meeting this transgender person and not knowing what to do or what to say to him.

Troy continues, "Anyway, the place we're going to is called Casablanca. Cesar is one of the best performers I have ever seen— And Chinua is so beautiful with this exotic smooth dark chocolate skin!" Troy exclaims, bouncing out of his seat, and then plopping down beside Erick. I roll my eyes, wondering when the day will come when people of color will no longer be exotic.

***

We meet Chinua for tea at the Rainbow Room cafe in The Village, twenty minutes later. He is every bit as beautiful as Troy had described.

I stir my chamomile tea, and look around the small café that is mostly inhabited by male couples. Across the room, the faucet behind the counter drips every few seconds. Biting my lower lip, I begin to think of Mama and hope that Mrs. Chapman is looking after her.

"So, Troy told us that you're working on your doctorate in Computer Science, with an emphasis in music software development?" Esperanza asks Chinua.

"Yea. I'll be done with my dissertation next term! Can't wait to bounce outta here."

"Troy said you actually sing opera, right?" Erick asks.

"It was my minor—vocal performance—at NYU. I figured that musicians are usually broke so why not pursue Computer Science?" he explains, sipping his latté.

"I love opera!" Erick exclaims. *Of course you do.*

"You should hear this guy tear up Don Giovanni. Simply heaven!" Troy beams, his crush now very apparent. I want to ask who or what a Don Giovanni is, but I am too embarrassed.

"I sang it for his birthday," Chinua tells us, smiling to Troy.

"You're from Nigeria, right? Ibo?" Esperanza asks with a coy smile.

"Wow, this girl is good!" he says, winking at her. He continues, "I was just an infant when we moved to New York City so I know my Brooklyn accent didn't give it away—"

"Chinua means 'God's own blessings' or something like that in Ibo, right?"

"Yea. My father named me. It's my middle name. Richard is my first name. Well, Chinua was my first name but my mother wanted me to be as Americanized as possible. She legally changed my name, once we moved here. It wasn't until my eighteenth birthday that I changed it back to my birth name."

"I hear you! My father gave me Amachi as a middle name—he was Ibo too—and my mother wanted my first name to be Esperanza. He used to call me Amachi all the time because he felt that Esperanza was too European. That's funny that you changed yours back, because I was thinking of doing the same thing for the anniversary of my father's death this summer."

Whenever Chinua's head is turned away from me, I sneak peeks of parts of his body, my eyes consuming chestnut colored fingers holding a spoon or a rich dark ear listening to Esperanza as she speaks. Each time I perform these secretive glances, my heart becomes exhilarated and I begin to wonder if he finds New York the sanctuary it has become for so many folks of color. I then begin to wonder about my own father and how it would have been if I had grown up with him in the house.

Eventually, he catches me taking a sneak peak at him. He grins and I look away at someone passing by our table. *Great, now he probably thinks I like him or something.* In the corner of the cafe, a female couple sits together, holding each other's hand, sharing a rather large milk shake. Within seconds, I envision that it is Esperanza and I sitting there. The fantasy lasts no longer than ten-seconds because Chinua's strong euphonic voice brings me back to reality.

"Your friend here just can't stop talking, can she?" Replying with a timid smile, my eyes avert to my now lukewarm tea.

"You should hear her in class. She can't stop talking," Erick tells him.

"Yea?" Chinua replies. Sniffing, I nod my head slightly, then look up, "Sorry, I'm just a little overwhelmed and exhausted and ain't never been to New York before."

"Sorry girl, I was just playin' wit cha. If you've never been here and you're coming from a small rural town, I know it must be a lot to take in. I'm playin' wit cha," he apologizes. I nod with a smile, assuring him that 'it's all good.'

"We had a long weekend. It was Savannah's birthday and she partied like it was 1999," Erick says. *Who says that still? It's 2007* ... I give him a deadly glance, translating to: if he values his life, he will not bring up my drunken lip lock with Esperanza.

"Well, happy belated birthday. How old?" Chinua asks.

"Nineteen. No biggie," I reply.

"It's always a big deal to be alive every year, every day, every minute, every second."

"He's always the epitome of optimism," Troy notes.

"She needs all the optimism she can get," Erick says.

"Screw you," I mouth under my breath.

***

"You remembered your fake I.D., right?" Esperanza asks me, a half hour later, as we walk down the street. "Of course I did." Her arm is linked through mine.

"You've been abnormally quiet ... I hope you aren't upset that we dragged you here. We really thought you'd enjoy it. I had no idea Troy's place would be like that."

"I'm not upset ... Just a little uncomfortable."

"Okay, just checking. Chinua is so sexy. I can definitely see why Troy is in love." The guys are walking ahead of us, Erick's arm around Troy's shoulder.

"They're so cute together. I see a possible hookup coming up shortly," she says.

"Troy and Erick? They broke up at the end of high school."

"That doesn't mean a thing. You saw how Erick was looking at him this morning." A fifty-something year old female couple passes by us and smiles.

"Why didn't you tell me you're changing your name to Amachi?" I finally ask her.

"Well, it's kind of a new idea. I was feeling guilty about changing it since my mother loves it so much. Toronto has quite the Nigerian population. I really started thinking about it when I started hanging out with them. I've also been thinking about my dad a lot too. You know I can be spontaneous, but I think I'm going to change it. You can still call me Esperanza, you know?"

I smile, "Good, because I think that's beautiful too." I step over something that looks like vomit on the sidewalk and cringe, "Why is this place so dirty!?" I exclaim.

"Come to Toronto! I swear, it's like a smaller and cleaner NYC."

"That stuff was nasty," I say, looking back at the spew on the sidewalk. I shutter at the thought of having almost stepped into another person's vomit.

"Yea, why is Erick wearing flip-flops? That's just some nastiness right there! What is up with white folk in the winter?" I exclaim.

"They do that craziness in Toronto too. Wearing shorts and sandals when there's snow on the ground," Esperanza points out with a giggle. Up ahead, Chinua turns around back towards us and says, "Esperanza, Savannah, hurry on up you two!"

"Sorry!" Esperanza exclaims as she forces me to skip faster in order to catch up with the men.

Amachi. Esperanza Amachi Perez.

As I semi-skip, semi-gallop towards the men, a breeze blows into our face, carrying indistinguishable fusion of fragrances from the millions of things and vibrant people, packed in every nook of this city.

Savi. Savannah. Savannah Penelope Sales.

I wonder what my father would have called me.

***

When we arrive at Casablanca, "Hey, Chinua is here!" is the greeting we receive from a rather tall Black woman wearing two afro puffs, a gold mini-dress, and very high sparkling platform shoes. Chinua hugs her, then kisses her on the cheek, "Looking beautiful as ever,

Mabel ... Everyone, this is Mabel Leen." Introductions are made, and as Mabel Leen gives me a hug, I cannot believe this feminine looking woman is in fact a man. A man!

"I'll be your waitress extraordinaire this afternoon," Mabel Leen tells us, followed by a cute little curtsy.

"Thanks," we say in unison. Chinua nods, then, turning back to Mabel Leen, he asks, "Is Cesar in the back?" Nodding, Mabel Leen replies, "Yes, getting ready."

"Thanks ... Listen, I'm going to say hello to him. I'll be at the table in about ten minutes, okay?" Chinua says. Patting him on the back, Troy replies, "Sure. See you in a bit."

"Wow, the women here are fabulous! Look at her leopard print dress over there. Look over there, a Carmen Miranda impersonator. She's beautiful!" Esperanza exclaims. However, all I can keep on thinking is, 'Esperanza, these aren't women, they're men!'

"We're the best in New York, girl," Mabel Leen says as we follow her to our table. It's smack right in front of the stage.

Great, I think with sarcasm.

"Great seats," Erick and Troy say together. They grin at each other and Troy says, "We're always on the same wavelength." Erick pulls Troy's chair out for him. Esperanza nudges me, "Hookup."

"Jesus I need a shot of something," I murmur, plopping down onto a red velvet upholstered chair next to Esperanza.

"It's not very crowded," I notice, looking around. About ten other patrons are scattered around the floor.

"We don't open for another fifteen minutes but y'all know Chinua and he's super special because he's best friends with Cesar ... Drinks?"

"So, what do you think so far?" Troy asks, several minutes later, sipping a chocolate martini that, for some reason, costs fifteen dollars. I roll my eyes, "A fifteen dollar martini, Erick?"

"Well, I offered you one since it was above your budget, but you said no," he says to me.

"It's not because it's above my budget. I said I didn't want one because that's obnoxious," I say. He decides to ignore me and then repeats the question to Esperanza, "So, what do you think?"

"Obnoxious isn't really the word I'd use as much as 'oblivious' to how many people have probably died to get that chocolate into your glass ..." Erick shakes his head, "Huh?—No, I mean, what do you think of the club so far?"

"Oh, you meant that," she says, shaking her head, pretending it was an innocent miscommunication, "I am so loving it! I love drag!"

A half hour later, Lady Chanel has just finished her rendition of "Anything Goes," one of Mama's favorite pieces. Our table is the loudest with applause and whistles. Lady Chanel blows us a kiss as she leaves the small stage.

"You guys enjoying yourselves?" Chinua asks, and then takes a bite from his Wasabi noodle and Shiitake mushroom dish.

"Hell yea!" Erick replies. Troy gives two thumbs up and Esperanza nods enthusiastically. I simply whisper, "Yes," and then continue chomping on my salad with too many carrots. I hate carrots.

"Cesar should be up next. I can't wait! He's got a new repertoire!" Chinua exclaims. The hostess of the night, Buttercup, introduces Cesar, "Ladies, gentlemen ... and other sorts ..." she pauses, then grins as the audience laughs.

"It pleases me to introduce to you, the electrifying, exhilarating and explosive, Cesar the Emperor!" The audience explodes with applause.

"He's quite popular here, eh?" Erick adds.

"You'll see why in a minute," Chinua replies with a grin. The lights on stage are dimmed, and the applause dies down. Seconds later, the music begins, and I instantly recognize it as James Brown's "I Feel Good."

"God, I love this song!" Esperanza exclaims.

"Everybody does," Troy says, clapping with the rest of the crowd. Out of nowhere, Cesar slides onto the stage on his knees. His outfit is just as catchy as his entrance: metallic blue bell-bottom pants with a matching long V-neck blue shirt and gold chain around his neck. As the music starts, I am amazed how much Cesar does sound like James Brown. So, he's really a woman? I don't understand. I'm confused.

"He's amazing!" Esperanza exclaims. As everyone nods in agreement, I am still trying to figure out how this Cesar is very convincingly a James Brown doppelganger. I am absolutely dumbfounded at this whole concept of gender bending. *It's a complete mind fuck,* I think to myself.

"Hey, you've been in there for a while, are you okay?" I hear Esperanza, twenty minutes later, as I sit on the toilet in Casablanca's bathroom. Cesar has just finished his performance, followed by a standing ovation. As soon as he had finished, I had gotten the sudden urge to rush to the bathroom.

"Savi?" Esperanza continues. I still don't reply. I should, but just don't feel like it at the moment.

"I know you're in here because those are your tacky orange Timberlands."

"I'm okay."

"Well, hurry up because Cesar's at our table and wants to meet everybody. I got an autographed picture too!"

"Tell him I'll be out in a minute."

"Are you really okay?"

"Sure."

"Okay, I'm heading back to the table. I'll get a signed picture for you just in case he runs out, okay?"

"Okay, thanks." About a minute later, I am washing my hands. I look up as an Asian woman—or maybe she's not a woman, who knows?—enters the bathroom. A few years older than me, she gives me a smile and says, "Cesar's great, huh?" I nod in agreement. She reaches into the inner pocket of her pink corduroy jacket, and then pulls out a matching pink scrunchie. Carefully lifting her red highlighted black hair into the air, she ties it back into a ponytail, quickly turns around, and then heads towards the last stall. On her way to the toilet, a thin cigarette falls from her outside coat pocket onto the lavender tiled floor. *Why is she smoking!?* My mind screams furiously. Instead of telling her that it has dropped from out of her pocket, I let her enter the stall.

Within a second, I am crushing the cigarette underneath my small foot, twisting and turning my ankle ferociously, smearing the white role with the hard heel of my rustic orange colored boot. For at least ten-seconds, I continue to kill it, smashing it as if it had been a diseased cockroach, on its way to infect an unsuspecting community; a melanoma, helping to feed an already broken world filled with an insurmountable number of broken bodies.

When I hear her flush the toilet, I catapult out of the women's bathroom like a vigilante in the night.

CHAPTER FIFTEEN

"Hi Mama, how are you?" I say.

"I'm fine, Savannah. You didn't have to call me again, baby. Where are you calling from?"

"Erick's cell phone. We're at some park ... You're okay?"

"Yes, honey. I hope you're having a good time, and not worrying about me. Ginger is coming over tonight. We gonna watch The Devil Wears Prada and Diary of a Mad Black Woman. Please, have fun and stop worrying about me. I'll be here when you get back."

"Promise me you aren't smoking while I'm away." I hear her pause for a moment, then answer, "I promise." I know that she is lying.

"Mama!"

"I only had one. Please don't get upset with me. It's just so hard. I only had one this morning—" she interrupts herself with a cough.

"That's why we bought you the Nicoderm."

"I promise I'll try not to have another one." I close my eyes, sigh, and command myself to be understanding, and to not make her feel bad.

"Now, go and have fun, okay? You don't have to call me every hour."

"Well, let me leave you Erick's cell phone number, just in case. He has voice mail on it."

"I already have the number of the house you at—"

"Please, please, please, Mama."

"If it will make you worry less about me—Wait a minute, I need to get something to write on." I turn around, and look about thirty feet in front of me. Cesar and Esperanza are sitting on a bench, laughing, while Erick, Chinua, and Troy are laying on the grass, looking up at the clear blue sky.

"Okay, I'm ready, baby," I hear my mother barely whisper. I give her the number, and make her repeat it to me, twice. I almost don't want to hang up as I hear her trying to suppress another cough while saying, "Goodbye baby. You have lots of fun for me, okay? Take lots of pictures."

"Sure ... I love you."

"I love you too. Now, hang up and have fun!" Then she is gone. I stare at the phone, wondering whether I should call her again.

"Everything okay back at the homestead?" I hear Erick ask. I turn around. He is right next to me.

"How long have you been there?"

"Chill, I didn't hear anything."

"Everything's fine. Thanks for letting me use your phone."

"No problem ... So, why haven't you talked to Cesar, yet?"

"I have," I lie. Great. I thought Esperanza was the only one who noticed. That means Cesar probably knows.

"Cut the crap. It's so obvious you're terrified of him."

"Go to hell Erick. I am not," I lie, slamming the cell phone into his palm.

"You'd think you'd be accepting of all minorities." My fists begin to clench, as I resist hitting him in the nose.

"Whatever, with your obnoxious freaking chocolate martini. Maybe you should ask Esperanza why any mention of coffee or chocolate pisses her off, before you start talking your 'we should treat everyone as equal,' spiel ... Just shut up," I reply.

"As usual, you respond with aggression. How do you even expect to begin some type of civilized dialogue with anyone when you're always so negative and angry all the freaking time?"

"I'm going to hit you." Erick rolls his eyes, "Ahhh! It's like talking to a bump on the log. Stop it!" He raises his arms in the air, hopelessly waiting for me to respond.

"I don't know why I am aggressive. I just am, goddammit! That's how I am. That's how I've survived."

"That's weak, Savannah. You're too intelligent to even let that become an excuse."

"That's right Erick, separate emotion from rational intelligence! God forbid if I digress back into the state of the emotionally volatile subhuman Negroid! Isa might not be intelligent no mo'—"

"Savannah, I didn't say any of that nonsense!"

"Whatever … can't we just go and have fun somewhere? That's why I'm here, right? To have fun and somehow forget that my life sucks and my mother is dying!" I yell, walking away from him, trying not to imagine Mama secretly lighting up a cigarette before Ginger comes by.

"Unbelievable!" I hear him say.

"What are you two arguing about, this time?" Esperanza asks me, several seconds later, as I sit down next to her. Cesar is now on the grass, talking to Troy and Chinua. I respond by putting my face in my hands, and then give her a muffled sigh.

"What'd you say to her, Erick?" I hear Esperanza ask as she begins to massage my tension-laden shoulders.

"I was civilized! You know how she can be aggressive when you're just trying to be nice to her," I hear Erick reply.

"I want to go home," I mumble through my hands.

"No you don't," Esperanza replies, patting me on the back, "We have a Broadway show to attend."

"What are you talking about?" I ask, uncovering my face. Erick is now sitting beside her.

"Annie. We're gonna see Annie. Cesar's got connections," she replies.

"I saw it in L.A. last year! It's about—" Erick begins.

"I know what it's about, Erick," I reply with a sigh of annoyance.

"Chill," he replies, rolling his eyes and shaking his head, "I was going to say, 'It's about time I see it again.' Stop yelling at me all the time. Why do you always have to be so mean to me!?" I make direct eye contact with him. Before I can yell at him again, I see in his eyes that I should stop and be the "better [wo]man." With reluctance, I tell myself to calm down and rationally explain to Captain America why I'm pissed off at this very moment.

"Sorry, I just get upset whenever I talk to my mother, okay? And she's smoking and she knows she shouldn't be doing that. I hear her fading away from me and it pisses me off. "

"I know sweetie, I know," Esperanza says.

"If you know this happens, then why don't you try to find another way to deal with it? Talk about the way you're feeling with

159

your friends, instead of barking at us?" Erick suggests. Rubbing my nose and letting out a sigh, "Because you do and say things that piss me off Erick. It's not just me. Like that martini nonsense. You have no idea why it was even hurtful to me and even more to Esperanza—"

"It's okay, Savi, the coffee and chocolate talk can be the next lesson. There was a time when you didn't know either," she whispers. How can she be so calm about everything he says and does? Okay, so there was a time, before I met Esperanza, I didn't know that people are still dying and enslaved for my Nestle Crunch or Hershey's bar. She's right, I reluctantly think to myself.

"Chocolate lesson? Huh? Do people of color, who are brown and Black, call themselves chocolate and coffee?" Erick asks, confused. I probably gave her the same look, too, during her first November in America, when I offered to share that Hershey's chocolate bar with her, during lunch, and she responded by crying about her father ... *Man, this is so hard. I know I'm not like him! I am not that oblivious.*

With a sigh, I explain, "Well, if you need to know, all I feel are intense emotions and I don't know how to verbally express myself in a way that you could possibly understand, without you thinking I'm a neurotic basket case. It's just that I know how I feel does matter and I just don't want to hold it in. I can't. I'm sorry, but that would kill me."

"Savannah, we already know you're a neurotic basket case. That's nothing new," Erick pipes, half joking, half serious.

"You're not making me feel any better, Erick," I reply.

"He's just joking," Esperanza says. Sniffing, I look over to where Cesar, Troy, and Chinua are. Cesar has his arm around Chinua's broad shoulders, and Troy is still lying down on the grass, pointing at the sky while saying something. Everyone then laughs, several seconds later. Several pigeons land in front of us then start pecking at pieces of food that people have dropped along the way. I turn my head to the left. Two young teenage girls whiz by on skates, holding hands and giggling, nearly skating into a middle-aged man who is walking two small dogs. Further down the street, a man is playing a guitar on a bench; a small crowd claps along, several toddlers running in and out of the circle, chasing each other.

"Would it really be good for me to live here? Would I really find myself or just lose myself here?" I mumble, looking down at the cobblestone path.

"What's she talking about?" Esperanza asks. Erick sits up straight, and then unfolds his hands, "The McEnroe."

"Huh?" she asks, with raised eyebrows. Shaking his head, "I guess she didn't tell you?"

"I didn't tell anybody else," I admit. Erick stands up, "Why not? Not even your mother?"

"If she knew …" I begin. He finishes for me, "She'd make you go? But, you feel obligated to stay home for the summer, to take care of her?"

"I don't feel anything! I am obligated to take care of her. Duh!"

"Savannah has the opportunity be a research assistant with a McEnroe fellow, in NYC this summer. All expenses paid," Erick tells Esperanza.

"And you were going to tell me this, when?" she asks with a suspicious eye, hands on her strong hips.

"I would have gotten to it, eventually," I lie.

"If you don't tell your mama, I will—"

"No!" I interrupt her.

"Savannah, do you know how good this would make her feel? To know this? You have to tell her. She deserves to know. Of all people, she deserves to know. "

"I know this, Esperanza. Let's talk about something else."

"Don't worry, Savannah Poo—"

"Erick, don't call me that." He grins, then says, "The sun'll come out …" and Esperanza continues, "Tomorrow. Bet your bottom dollar …" and Erick finishes, "that tomorrow, there'll be sun." Rolling my eyes, I can't help but to grin, "What did I do to deserve such corny and cheesy friends?"

***

I sit through Annie and try to lose myself in the story and sappy music. However, throughout the entire show, I can't help but to think of the mere fact that this poor little orphan girl suddenly is swept up into the wealthy world of Daddy Warbucks. Suddenly, all her problems are solved and she can obtain any dream she wants because Daddy Warbucks can buy it. This isn't a happy ending and it isn't reality.

"Only you could ruin such an American classic," Erick tells me, shortly after we have left the musical. We are all now riding on the Metro, back to Troy's place, and I have just expressed my 'issues' with Annie. We pass by an advertisement for Oprah Winfrey's production, The Color Purple. Why the hell didn't we see that instead?

"People don't necessarily go to Broadways or movies for reality, Savannah. They go to lose themselves in fantasy. I know it's not reality. I come in with that mindset. I appreciate other stuff like choreography and vocal performance. Those are some talented little girls," Esperanza explains. I am sitting in between them, while Troy, Chinua, and Cesar sit to Erick's left.

"I've never heard of anyone having problems with Annie," Troy says to me.

"Remember, Savannah's specialty is all about the glass being half empty," Erick says. I shrug and reply, "Whatever. Everyone's entitled to their own opinions of entertainment."

"She doesn't listen," Erick tells Troy.

"I listen. It's just, why is Daddy Warbucks so great, anyway? He probably made all his money through sweatshops, slaves, and promoting economic imperialism. He adopting Annie wasn't out of love—"

"Stop being miserable and complaining! You got to see your first Broadway for free for Christ's sake!" Erick nearly yells.

"I'm not being miserable, I'm making a social commentary!" I yell back. Everyone in the group is quiet, suddenly; all eyes drawn to Erick and I.

"Do we have to separate you two?" Chinua intervenes with a grin. Erick shakes his head, rolls his eyes, then sighs, "I mean, this is getting old, Savannah! Chinua, what Esperanza and I are simply trying to do is make her understand that life doesn't have to be miserable. But she keeps on perceiving things just the same old negative way. It's like she can't be happy unless she's miserable; unless she can find misery in everything. You're not the only one on this planet that is suffering for shits sake!"

I bite my lower lip and refrain from punching him.

"Come on, people are staring," Esperanza says.

"I don't care. This immature crap with your attitude has got to stop right now, or by the time you are twenty-five, you're not going to have any freaking friends left that care about you!" The train stops. Cesar calmly announces, "Children, this is our stop."

We all pause for a moment, and then Cesar makes his way to the exit. Quietly, we all follow. Huffing to myself, I wonder how much longer I can resist punching him in the mouth, ruining that disgustingly perfect row of lily-white straight teeth.

"You know, yelling at her isn't helping," I hear Esperanza whisper to Erick, a few feet in front of me.

"Sorry, it's just that she's the first person I've ever befriended that can make me lose my cool in a matter of seconds," he explains. Esperanza puts her arm around his shoulders, "Just chill, sweetie, it takes two to Tango. She isn't trying to give you an ulcer."

"Sometimes I wonder. I'm just trying to be good! My intentions are good, dammit." I hear him say. I am about to scream to him, "The road to hell is paved ..." when Esperanza calmly says, "And that's the problem ..."

I drop back a few paces to lose earshot of the conversation. Hearing anymore will cause me to overheat and explode. Drenched in months of unpaid overtime, I have just punched out my timecard, and am officially passing the buck onto her.

***

I am not crazy. Maya knows. bell, can I get an amen? Nina, sing it! I am not wrong and certainly not crazy. I'm passionate about being heard, not just seen. I do not see misery in everything. I see how beautiful things have been made miserable.

I scrutinize the inscription that I have just written, on the inside cover of Maya Angelou's *I Shall Not Be Moved*. It is about an hour later and we are back at the 'estate,' lounging in the living room, listening to Simon and Garfunkel on the Bose audio system. Erick and I haven't spoken to each other since leaving the subway.

While everyone has congregated on the right side of the room, I have found a comfortable leather beanbag chair to sit on at the other end of the room. I am sipping a Dos Equis and pretending to read my book of Maya Angelou's poetry that I had brought for the train ride.

"Maya knows," I whisper. I read the passage several times in a faint whisper, slowly nodding my head back and forth to the Nina Simone song, "Images," which is archived in my memory and replaying to mask the Simon and Garfunkel. After reciting my words for the fourth time, I end the chant with the last line of Nina, ."..and dishwater gives back no image." Memories of Mama's first job in Lebanon as a dishwasher and janitor, at East Lebanon public school, also spin around in my memory bank. Mama, whose spirit is beautiful, body made miserable in this world.

I am not crazy.

"I used to read Maya with my mother when she or I was having a bad day. She used to say, 'Maya is my girl! That sistah just gets it.'" As I look up from my state of hopelessness, Cesar's chocolate brown irises greet me. How the hell did he just read my mind?

He sits down beside me, and then continues, "You ever listen to Nina while reading Maya? It's as if they were married to each other in a past life as soul mates—or maybe they were sisters?" For the first time in hours, a smile slowly finds its way to each corner of my mouth and the anxiety about finally talking to him slowly melts away.

"I had contemplated being a Nina Simone impersonator, years ago, before I found Cesar in me. You know why I didn't?" I shake my head innocently, his sandalwood cologne filling my nostrils. I am reminded of Davis.

"The first night I ever performed professionally was at this fancy expensive club, in Manhattan, called Ivory. It was 1995 and I was twenty-five years old. I had come to the stage ready with a full civil rights-themed Nina Simone repertoire. I had studied and practiced Nina's songs for years; complete with over twenty years of piano training and goddamn it I was eager to share Nina's soul! Goddess bless her heart! The curtain opened, and there, sitting before me was an audience filled with New York City's wealthiest patrons—all white and pristine, indicative of the clubs name. You know what I ended up singing that night?"

"Nina Simone," I answer. He continues, "Until that point, I had only shared Nina with my family during the holidays. We'd all get together in the living room and I'd play the piano and sing. My grandmother used to cry when I'd finish 'Strange Fruit' because her first son had been lynched before I was born." He pauses for a second, interlocks his long dark brown fingers into each other, looks down, and then grins to himself, "Nina, Maya ... Audre—you know Audre?"

"I've heard of her but haven't read her yet." He nods, "Nina, Maya, Audre—these were the women I shared with my mother, after a day of someone calling her a 'nigger' or after a day of coming home from school, crying because I had escaped yet another boy calling me a 'dyke' for not letting him touch me. This was the mid 80's in Mississippi, mind you. You ever been to 'Sippi? That's what my grandfather calls it. He was always saying, 'When you comin' home to 'Sippi again, Renee?' every time I would call him and sing to him on his birthday. He and my father never did get used to calling me Cesar ..." He gingerly removes the book from my hand. With beautiful finesse, he caresses the cover with his right index finger.

"These sistahs spoke for us ... to us. We who suffered didn't just know what they were speaking about; we felt what they were speaking about, viscerally. When it came to Nina, we didn't know it as trendy nostalgia or high fashion entertainment.

"That night, on the cusp of my first professional performance, I thought that Nina's pearls of wisdom are priceless to us; not to be cast out to people who are not ready to learn from it ..." He pauses again and my eyebrows lift in anticipation for him to finish the recollection of his first night at Ivory.

"Forty minutes after the curtain opened, I received a standing ovation for my repertoire of the Cole Porter songbook instead, Nina safely tucked away with the intimate memories of sharing and learning with my mother." Erick laughs from across the room as Troy points to something in the XY magazine they are both reading through. Cesar lift's his head, looks at them for a brief moment, then turns to me, eyes crisp with love and sincerity, "They're cute together, eh?" I shrug in response, "I guess." He looks back down at the book and then opens it to the first page. As he reads my scribbled inscription, he grins as if he had written it himself.

Erick giggles again and I look across the room. He looks at me as well, offers me a tentative smile, waves, then mouths, "Hi." He continues to wave his hand as if it were a white flag. I return the gesture with a half-smile.

Closing the book, he then places it in front of me. "Troy, Erick—they ain't bad people ..." he pauses, looks down at the floor for several seconds, then continues, "...but sometimes we all make assumptions. With the folk at Ivory, I ended up not singing Nina to them because I had thought, 'Most of them don't realize they ain't quite ready to listen to the gift of truth from her soul.'"

"They'll never be ready," I whisper, pessimistically shaking my head. We both look across the living room, momentarily interrupted by Esperanza who is giggling at something Chinua has said.

"I can see why you are in love with her. Her spirit is bright enough to light up all of New York City at night." How did he know?

"I bet you've learned a lot about yourself because of her, huh?" I nod, smiling, "Still learning ... I wish I could say the same thing about the other one." I sigh, shaking my head as my eyes move from Esperanza's mouth to Erick's face.

"You've learned nothing?" he asks. I am unable to tell if he is being sincere or sarcastic. He's being sarcastic, right? I roll my eyes, shaking my head, "I've learned nothing and will never learn nothing from him," anger lacing every word. He tilts his head slightly to the left, "Sweetheart, then why are you here with him, in New York, since both of you seem to think that neither one of you are particularly ready to listen to each other's soul?" I give him a curious look, tilting my head to the side. *Okay, so he can read me like a book.* However, I reply defensively, "Let's get this straight: I listen to him all the damn time. I listen to how he doesn't get it. I'm here because I'm dumber than a box of rocks." I look down at my book, sigh, then repeat in a low whisper, "Dumber than a box of rocks."

"It's not stupidity. You're both simply not ready to receive the gifts from each other's souls yet—"

"That man is so vapid. What gift?"

"You've given each other a lot more than you'd like to admit. Not all gifts come in the form of an Esperanza. If that were the case, we'd never struggle and learn about ourselves in the most deepest and intense ways possible. A beautiful struggle is a gift. Yea, when you're in it you don't quite see it that way—"

"That's for goddamn sure 'cause I don't see what you're talking about." Okay, that's a half-truth. I know I'm grappling with denial of the pure truth of what he is saying.

"It will happen when it happens … But, you know why you're here. There is something satisfying and powerful about the place you are at in here, right now," he points to his heart then continues, "We've all been there before. Well, most of us. We have the power to make tremendous change in the hearts of those that we feel would otherwise continue to make us, and our children, suffer. We are a mirror and what we reflect to each other is often unsettling."

"Well, somebody's gotta do it! He's twenty-seven years old and he claims I was the first person to accuse him of doing the white male privilege bullshit. If I don't do it, then he's going to make tons of folk miserable! And look at him over there! He's all relaxed and whatnot. He doesn't even care that he's making me insane."

"Don't let him fool you. Every time that boy looks at you, he sees a mirror and he is scared that he is that person you have accused him of being. You're probably feeling the same thing when you look at him."

"Sorry Cesar, but I will not be this man's emotional mammy just because he feels guilty, every time he looks at a brown or Black person."

"But that's why you stay, Savannah."

"Huh?" I ask in confusion.

"Not to be a mammy, but a mirror. No matter how frustrating it has been, you like being that mirror. Right now, you like that he feels something unique when he looks at you in particular, because maybe this is something that has never happened to him; not until he met you." Cesar pauses for a long ten seconds, gently humming what sounds like "Summertime." He taps my nose with his right index finger and whispers, "It's a power you've never experienced before." *Power? What power?*

He continues, this time raising his voice a little louder while keeping his tone gentle, "At this point on your path, you don't quite know what to do with it, but you know you cannot abandon it. That's why you stay. Something in your soul is telling you to stay; to make it through this beautiful struggle. It's not about being dumber than a box of rocks. It's not about being smart. It's something deeper and without words." My toes curl up tightly as I resist the urge to cover my ears and leave the room.

"Nah, impossible," I lie to him ... and myself.

"And it intrigues you, yet, simultaneously scares you right now. After all, I'm pretty sure you've never fathomed a close relationship with this type of person, before. You've surprise and scared yourself."

"Please, what do I have to be scared of?" I ask with a shrug. He smiles affectionately, seeing through my façade.

"It's fear of our own power and potential to affect change that holds so many of us back. Our gifts not only teach those rare few who are ready to listen, we also know we'll learn a lot of unexpected things about ourselves from them; often, things that will scare us: 'Am I actually capable of loving my enemy?' 'Am I hearing the very soul of the person I thought could only hurt me?'

"It's difficult to know when we're supposed to share our wisdom and our gifts, because they certainly aren't meant for everybody, you know? That night at Ivory, I was young, inexperienced, and excited ... but scared. Now that I look back, it wasn't my spirit telling me, 'These pearls shall be cast. But not here and not now.' It was fear. If you listen to your spirit, you'll feel when it is the right time. It could be tomorrow, it could be five years from now—"

"Uh, no. There is no way I want Erick in my life for five more days. He does not deserve my pearls."

"Well, do you deserve his?"

"He has nothing to offer me." However, I cannot fool myself as memories of him bringing me to the café when I came out, letting me sleep in his bed when I was drunk, and giving me those pamphlets, try to creep into my conscience and consciousness. *Whatever, those weren't pearls. It was just pity ...*

"Two years ago, I was invited to perform at Ivory for their seventy-fifth year anniversary. Girl, I hadn't been there in ten years. Debra Thompson, the new director, had seen me perform and wanted me to do several James Brown songs. It had been a tough month for me, and I wasn't sure I wanted to be bothered. Katrina had just hit Mississippi. My mama and sis had to relocate to Florida to live with my father's side of the family. I had just arrived back in New York, after having helped my mama and sister move. I had been in a café in Manhattan, relaxing before my performance by reading Octavia Butler's *Kindred*—"

"I loved that book!"

She smiles, "I'm thinking of turning it into a musical. Am working something out with Chinua. Anyway, I remember I was in that cafe, and this very white and very rich male couple was sitting in front of me, talking about what they thought about Katrina. Long story short, they concluded that those people down there were, 'really stupid for not leaving before the hurricane hit' and maybe they 'just stayed to loot their own city.'"

"Oh damn. What did you do?"

"Oh, the story isn't over. One of them said, 'Let's get the check, I want to get to Ivory's anniversary cocktail party before the show starts.'

"I remember thinking to myself, 'Didn't I go through this nonsense in 1995? Why am I going back there?' After hearing that, the last thing I wanted to do was sing at Ivory. But then, there I was, three hours later, walking out onto the stage in my James Brown outfit ...and there were those two men from the cafe, sitting in the front row, holding hands, right in the front for me to see. Fear wanted me to leave, but my spirit told me to stay. I walked to the piano with my head held high, sat down, and put my black fingers on those glossy ivory keys. The first song I was supposed to sing was "I Feel Good." But I didn't feel good at all, and that wasn't the song I wanted to sing. My daddy, who passed away five years ago, spoke to me. I heard him say, "Renee, the pearls shall be cast." I opened my mouth, hit the keys, and Mississippi Goddamn came rolling out, except I replaced every instance of the word 'Mississippi' with 'Katrina,' and played it slowly instead of quickly so they could feel every word. My second song was Nina's rendition of 'Take Me to the Water,' except I sang 'Save Me from the Water.' My third and final song was 'Strange Fruit.' 'Southern seas bear strange fruit, blood on the levees and blood at the root, Black bodies drowning in the southern breeze. Strange fruit floating in Katrina's seas,'" he coos to me. I shiver as images of Katrina's wrath fill my mind.

"As I breathed out that last line of the song, I just lost it and started crying on stage. Without shame, I told them I was mourning for my mama's lost home that my late daddy had built with his brother; those floating bodies; the days of misery in the Superdome; and our people as still being seen as 'nothing but a nigger' by many of New York's most refined and civilized. I looked towards that couple from the café, and they were bawling. I looked that couple in the eyes, and then one of them mouthed back, 'I am sorry. I am so sorry.' And his eyes told me he meant it. My anger and rage had melted away, and I was there, on stage, watching a majority of the audience reveal their soul to me through tears they probably hadn't expected to shed. This country has so much pain. So much un-reconciled fear and hate amongst each other ... and towards our own selves.

"On that stage, I sang without judgment; without feelings of guilt that I was sharing my gift outside of my family ... and without feeling pleasure from the guilt and sorrow that my truthsong had illicit from the crowd. I sat there, on stage, giving and receiving the gift of tears. That night, I had sung truth to power, letting them know that healing, for all of us, is possible."

***

Several minutes later, with the voice of melodic sincerity, Cesar has persuaded me to come hang out with everyone else. I am not sure how he did it, but here I am, sitting beside Esperanza, drinking my third beer, silently thinking about Cesar's truthsong to me, realizing I'm quite inebriated. *Okay, so what do I do with it?* I sigh, *This sucks.* It sucks because deep in my heart, I simply cannot contest one thing Cesar has said. Why couldn't he make it simple and say, "You're right Savi, class privileged white people suck. I don't even know why you're bothering with this Erick fellow," or, "Why should you take on the burden of educating some white guy about his whiteness? Don't you have better things to do?"

"Music change!" Esperanza exclaims, bouncing up from off of the sofa, and then rushing towards the stereo system. Removing her iPod from her bag, she looks at me and says, "I need me some Lila Downs! What about you, girl!?"

"Who's that?" Chinua asks, shifting his weight on the leather beanbag chair he's sitting on.

"I think she's the chick that sang in the movie Frida, right?" Troy asks.

"And so much more! Where do I plug this puppy in!?" Esperanza exclaims with a giggle.

Troy gets up, "Let me help you there, little missy." Now it is just Erick and I on the sofa. I drink the rest of my beer as he decides to move right next to me, "Hey, what's up?"

I shrug in reply. *Why would I want to love him?*

"Does that mean you're still mad at me?" *And learn exactly what from him?*

"No. Yes … kind of. I don't know." I look down and fiddle with a loose string on my clothes. I let out a deep sigh of emotional and physical exhaustion. Lila Downs's Una Sangre album starts playing. Sitting next to each other silently, we watch as Esperanza dances with Troy to "Viborita." A minute later, Chinua and Cesar have joined them.

What could possibly be 'deep' about Erick? Gift? Yea, the gift of irritation.

Finally, Erick breaks the silence between us, "I'm sorry. I thought you'd have a good time here." Again, I shrug in response and then reach over to get a glass bottle of some imported mineral water I've never heard of.

"I just didn't really think about how uncomfortable you'd be at Troy's place, until we arrived. It's just such a nice place, I kind of forgot that maybe you'd think differently about it."

"You don't have to feel sorry for me or the shanty my mother and I live in," I reply, half-jokingly, raising my head up to look him in the eyes. A smile tries to find its way to my full lips.

"No, really Savi," he begins, sighs, and then continues, "Sometimes I just forget stuff like this, but I'm trying not to. The other day, when I was at Whole Foods, I realized for the first time that the patrons there are almost all white, and most of the people working there are Black or brown."

"Did Esperanza talk to you or something?" I ask, shaking my head in disbelief that he could have possibly had this insight on his own.

"No, Savi." I roll my eyes, "Are you lying that she didn't help you out of your selective amnesia? It didn't seem to 'come to you' when you ordered those two ridiculously expensive martinis and thought nothing of it." He crumples his eyebrows, eyes shifting back and forth, thinking about what to say next.

"Okay, I guess I'm annoying you. I'm going to go brush my teeth in the third floor bathroom and go to bed."

"Have fun," I reply dryly, opening the bottle of water. He tells everyone he's off to bed and then heads upstairs. A minute or so passes by. *Stop being a mean bitch, Savi—*

I am not being a mean bitch—Oh stop! What the hell did he do wrong? When he doesn't bring up class and race you get pissed. Now when he tried to talk about it, you get pissed—

I interrupt the battle between my thoughts with a growl, take a deep breath, and then reluctantly decide to go to the third floor bathroom.

"Hey," I greet him as he's brushing his pearly whites. He spits into the marble sink, "You actually want to talk to me now?"

"Maybe." I give him a sincere smile, and he can't help but to grin. Shaking his head, he then points to me, "You."

"You what?" He begins gargling some water. I tickle him in the stomach playfully, catching him off guard. He quickly spits in the sink before he starts laughing.

"What was that? You actually made playful contact with me. Are you flirting with me?"

"Of course."

"I don't get it. One minute you hate me and the next minute you're my best friend."

"I don't hate you ... I admit it, I have some issues, Erick."

"Well, have you considered that you could be manic depressive or something?"

"I'm poor, that's my problem. Nothing money can't really solve."

"Money doesn't solve everything. Trust this privileged white boy on that one," he says with a wink. He wipes his mouth clean with a white towel.

"Oh, so the mere fact that my mother is dying from emphysema, or that I can only afford to go to a community college, or that I've had a painful cavity for the past year that I can't afford to have filled has nothing to do with the fact that my life sucks?"

"I don't know Savi ... You've just got so much going for you and you don't see it. Dr. Rogards sees how promising you are. You're a freshman and he offered you the McEnroe. That's going to open a floodgate of opportunities that you've been looking for."

"But you know I can't take the damn thing—"

"That's not true. I don't believe the reasons you've given me are valid enough to not take it."

"Okay, I really try to be open-minded when I talk to you, but the things that come out of your mouth are so oblivious to how things really are, Erick. I cannot take this stupid fellowship. Period. If you have realistic and helpful suggestions about who is going to take care of my mama, I'm listening."

"Well, I just don't think I would always be angry, Savi, that's all I'm saying. Seriously, has your constant anger made you any happier? I wouldn't be angry all the time, that's all I'm saying."

"That's so easy for you to say, Erick."

"Why do you think that?"

"Sorry, but it's called a layer cake of privilege. Stop pretending we are the same. At least admit that it's made your life easier."

"Okay, easier, but not necessarily happier."

"Like there is a difference."

"There is."

"Erick, my mother is dying. My only concept of family is dying."

"You're scared of losing your mom. Who isn't? I understand that, but why let fear prevent you from going to New York City this summer? I know it's been hard for you to deal with a fatal disease, but—"

"Do you really?" He presses his lips together, and tries to figure out what to say next, but seems lost for words.

"No, you don't. Erick, do you know what it's like to literally not know what the following week will bring? Do you know what it's like to wake up next to your mother's bedroom, every morning, and thank God that she is still breathing? That she hasn't died in her sleep and left you alone? Do you know how it feels to know whether death will creep into your life, tomorrow, ending the life of the one person that has kept you going!?" At this point, I have lost control of my voice and am yelling at him—

—I jump in surprise as Erick hits the countertop with his right fist, then takes something out of his pocket and hurls it past my head. I hear whatever it is, shatter against the back wall.

"Why are you always fucking yelling at me!? You don't think it kills me, every time I realize I do or say something that hurts you!? You're so selfish!" He screams at the top of his lungs. Before I can yell something back at him, he surprises me by exploding into tears, collapsing to the floor, and burying his face into his left hand. My mouth gapes wide open and nothing comes out. Suddenly, my frustrations with him melt away. I kneel in front of him and then try pulling his hand away from his face, "I'm sorry Erick. I didn't mean to make you cry!" I belt out. His hand remains pressed up again his face. I take my hands away from him as I hear him mutter, "Fuck off." I stand up quickly, about to run out of the bathroom—but then I don't. My heart barks back at me, "You better stay the hell right there, Savannah."

"Just leave me alone," he chokes through tears. Tears begin welling in my own eyes as I literally step back from myself and watch Erick fall apart right in front of my eyes. His slender frame begins trembling as his tears become more intense and his strong body transitions into a fetal position.

Wiping my own tear-streaked face with my hands, I look away from Erick and notice that yellow colored pills are scattered across the beautifully blue and lime tiled floor. Beside Erick's head is a plastic prescription bottle: the object he had taken from his pocket and thrown. I pick up the bottle and read the label on the bottle—

—"Oh God," I choke, dropping the small container to the floor. Erick continues sobbing and trembling ...

... I find myself on the floor, crying uncontrollably as well. Lying on my side, I am mirroring my friend's body, his hand still covering his eyes and nose, sobbing through words that I cannot yet understand. My left hand is holding his hot neck, my forehead pressed against his, and my small right palm is pressed up against his rapidly pounding heart ...

... little yellow pills of Abacavir, scattered throughout the bathroom ...

***

March 24, 1992

"What the fuck do you want?" Mama says the 'fuck' word all the time. I don't know what it means. When she is angry, she says it all the time. I am not allowed to say it.

"Mama?" I call to her, trying to fix my purple party birthday hat. Beside me is a red party hat for Davis. It is my fourth birthday and I think Davis should wear a red hat. It's his favorite color. Mama says he'll be here any minute, but I don't know how long that is. On the coffee table, there is a tray of carrot cupcakes with white frosting and orange sprinkles. Mama is the best cupcake maker in the world. She always puts extra carrots in it because I like carrots.

"Leave, Scott. You are not welcomed here," I hear Mama say. I think she is at the front door. The doorbell rang and I wanted it to be Davis. But Mama said 'fuck.' She is angry because it is not Davis. It is a boy named Scott. I never invited a boy named Scott. It is only Davis and his mama and daddy that I invited to my party.

"Lily, I just wanted to stop by. Haven't seen you in five years—"

"God damn it, how the hell did you find us? Don't ever come back here!" I hear Mama yell. My heart starts beating fast as I get up quickly to see if Mama needs my help. I run towards the front doorway and see Mama, in her white dress with yellow and blue polka dots, trying to close the door so Scott doesn't come in. Mama's chocolate brown legs are shaking as she tries to close the door. I rush up and then try to push the door to help her.

"No Savi, go to the bedroom and lock the—" Scott pushes his way through the door and I fall onto the floor. I look up and see a big white man with a shaven head and light brown eyes. He smells like the stuff Mrs. Chapman's husband drinks when she babysits me, except it is really strong and I do not like it or the strange smile he gives me.

"Is it someone's birthday today?" I answer with a timid nod, then back away from him. Mama moves in between us, "God damn it, leave right now ... Savi, go to the bedroom—"

"I just came by to see if you needed some money," he tells Mama. His words sound funny; like he is talking with too much peanut butter in his mouth. I back away from both of them but am too scared to leave Mama.

"We don't need your help. We don't need a damn thing from you. I got a good job at the school—"

"I went to jail because of you. I loved you." The big scary man coughs several times, but he does not cover his mouth like you're supposed to so you don't spread germs. His jeans and blue coat are very dirty; like he was playing in the mud. I like playing in the mud but I take my muddy clothes off before I come inside.

"You need to go before I call the cops." He is so big and scary; much bigger than Mama who is very skinny. He grabs Mama's arm, slams the door behind him, and then throws her down to the floor beside me. No one hurts my mama. No one!

I jump up, run towards him, and then punch him in his pee-pee as hard as I can. I know this hurts because Davis told me that that hurts boys a lot and that I should never do it to him.

"That isn't any way to treat your daddy." Scott isn't my daddy. Why would he tell me that? Mama said my daddy's in Georgia.

Instead of crying from being punched in the pee-pee, Scott laughs at me. Mama jumps up, pulls me back, and yells, "Go to the bedroom and lock—"

He hits her in the face. Boys aren't supposed to hit girls, but Scott hits Mama hard in the face. I scream and start to run towards our bedroom—

—My head feels like there is bubbles in it … Darkness …

… What was I doing? Oh yea, it's my birthday. Did I fall asleep while waiting for Davis? That's silly of me—

—Mama. Mama needed my help! I open my eyes as fast as I can. For some reason, I am laying on the carpet. I try to stand up, but my legs are frozen. Why can't I move? My head begins to hurt and I notice I cannot hear anything. I put my hand on my forehead. It feels like there is water on my head. Why is there water on my head? I didn't take a bath. I look at my hand and I see that the water is red.

"Mama!" I scream, turning around slowly as I remember she was near the front door with that scary man. I grab the edge of the coffee table to pull myself up. My head feels like there are heavy bubbles in it again, but I try not to go back to sleep. Mama needs my help.

But Mama and Scott are not at the front door anymore.

I throw up my morning breakfast of birthday pancakes that Mama made with M&Ms and marshmallows. Throw up always smells funny. On all fours, like a kitty cat, I am staring down at my throw up and see a few M&Ms. The bubbles in my head become heavier. "Don't … sleep now," I tell myself, crawling towards our bedroom, looking for Mama. I notice that I am beginning to hear again. My ears follow weird sounds and I slowly crawl towards the kitchen, "Mama, I hurt my head," I whisper, red water dripping onto the floor. I hear weird noises that sound like grunting. I crawl around the corner, towards the kitchen where the sounds are coming from. I think they are behind the counter.

Scott's pants are pushed down his legs and he is on top of Mama, making strange grunting noises. Mama's eyes are closed and her nose has red water under it.

I am screaming. Bubbles become heavier in my head and I can no longer move although I want to help Mama. The bubbles become too heavy and I fall asleep …

… Mr. Allen is holding my hand. He is looking down at me and smiling. His eyes are watery and I think he is crying. But how can that be? He is smiling so why would he be crying? I like when he smiles because he looks exactly like Davis. Why is Mr. Allen holding my hand?

"Do you want a cupcake? I picked out the frosting," I whisper, wondering where Davis is and why Mama hasn't come yet to help me fix my party hat. Why am I laying on my back?

"Is my party hat okay?" I whisper. He is pressing down on my forehead with something soft.

"Are you helping me with my party hat? Is it okay?"

"It's perfect. You look like a princess." Mr. Allen says. I want to ask him where Davis is, but he starts sounding like he is far away … really far away … I am feeling sleepy and feel like I'm falling into the bubbles …

… Darkness.

***

March 27, 2007
Dear Diary,

2:07 P.M.
Those little pills …
Those little yellow pills. I don't think I can write about this … I don't know how to write about this.

2:27 P.M.
Little yellow pills of Abacavir. Albuterol, and oxygen tanks.
My scar. Erick's scars. Mama's scars. Too many scars.
(Sorry it's so messy, diary. My hands just won't stop shaking)

3:32 P.M.
"... I still feel the pain, every fifteenth of the month. I'm twenty-one again. It's 2000, August 15th, 2:15 am. I remember the putrid smell of the alley, the knife, the pain, blood ... him tearing into me, trying to be inside of me ... I will never un-remember his words ... they made me remember everything."

***

Closing my journal, I sigh as the New York City train enters the city of Hartford, Connecticut. We will be at the station soon. Erick stirs beside me, waking up from his slumber. Esperanza sits across from us, bobbing her head to whatever is playing on her iPod, reading her book, *Refreshing Pauses: Coca-Cola and Human Rights in Guatemala.*

Erick greets me from his nap by taking my left hand, squeezing it gently, and whispering, "Hey."

"Now entering Hartford Union Station!" The conductor exclaims from the middle of the aisle. I put my hand on top of Erick's and then respond with a long, deep sigh.

"Everything will be okay. I can feel it," he tells me with a confident but tired smile. We both had not slept at all last night. Memories had rolled off our tongues all night long and into the early morning.

The train comes to a complete stop.

Nearly two decades ago, the same station had greeted a nineteen-year-old named Lily Mae Sales, as she had exited from a bus after a long and arduous trip from Georgia.

I am returning to East Lebanon, to my two-bedroom apartment, to my mama ...

... and to myself.

"Homecoming," I whisper.

CHAPTER SIXTEEN

My hand is shaking as I give mama the two postcards I had bought for her from New York City.

"Thanks baby, I was hoping you wouldn't forget," she says, as she takes them, walks over to the refrigerator, and then sticks them next to the other postcards we have received from the Davis' many vacations. Mama loves collecting postcards.

"Where should I put this tacky orange thing?" Davis asks. I turn around and then sign for him to put my duffel bag in my bedroom. Davis had picked me and Esperanza up from Erick's place. He had first driven Esperanza home, and then me. He doesn't know that I know and that I remember everything.

"Shouldn't you be using your oxygen, Mama?" Her tank is next to the kitchen table where she was reading Essence magazine. I slowly enter the kitchen, taking deep breaths, *This is where it happened. Right there, in front of the sink—*

"I don't think I need it every minute ... Greenwich Village? That's where those gay folk live, right?" She asks, looking at the postcard with Stonewall on the front. I continue breathing deeply, feeling my stomach begin to twist and turn at the very thought of confronting her with my newfound memories. What if I give her an anxiety attack and it hurts her lungs? But I have to tell her. It's hurting me too. She always asks me to tell her if I remember.

"Yup, that's the spot. We saw a drag show. A James Brown impersonator. I think you would have really liked it. I took lots of pictures."

"Is Davis staying for dinner? I hope he's staying for dinner. I made plenty of fried chicken, beans, and onion rings. I know you like onion rings. Did you get a picture of Ground Zero?" I look at the kitchen floor, my own ground zero, several feet away from me, and then whisper, "Nope. That's not really something I want to take a picture of." Her back, clothed in a Baby Phat magenta colored tee shirt that I had bought her for her birthday last year, faces me. She shifts her slim body to the left, and then cocks her head slightly to the right, rearranging the postcards on the refrigerator, in order to find an appropriate place for the new additions. She's standing right in that place.

"Why didn't you tell me?" I mouth to her back. I feel sadness, heartbreak, and hopelessness pulsating through my blood; her blood and his.

I touch the scar on my head then bite down on my lower lip. *The memory of that white ogre on top of her limp brown body has forever replaced the mythic picture I had of a father. My father was supposed to be a light-skinned Black man with a big afro and baritone Southern drawl, born and raised somewhere in Georgia. Maybe she doesn't remember what happened. Maybe they told her what happened, but she never saw it because she was unconscious. Not like me. Maybe I shouldn't tell her. Maybe my amnesia was protecting her and that meant she was able to protect me. Maybe she doesn't know I saw it—*

"Hey, I'm talking to you, geek!" I hear Davis say rather loudly, startling me. For a few seconds, I had forgotten that he is here.

"You've been acting weird ever since I picked you up. Did you get hammered again?" he signs to me with a silly grin. He then imitates someone who is in a drunken stupor.

"No ..."

"So, I was asking if we're going to look at the pictures from New York, tonight? I brought my MacBook so you can download them."

"Sure. After dinner. Mama wants you to stay for dinner. Can you?"

"Of course I can stay for dinner! What kind of question is that?" he exclaims. He takes off his black wool coat, and then hangs it on the coat hook beside the front door.

"Good. You two want to eat now?" she asks, back still turned to us, taking a postcard with an image of the Florida Keys on it, and moving it to the opposite side of the refrigerator.

"I don't know why everyone wants to move to Florida when they retire. So damn hot and humid with a trillion goddamn mosquitoes, I'd take a cold New England winter day over that mess anytime," she says. Finally, she turns around to face us, "So, how was the trip? Gimme details while I fix us some plates." She glides from that place to the stove, where there are the same two cast iron pots and a skillet we've had since I can remember. Pulling two plates from off of the shelf above, she exclaims, "I burned the beans a bit, but they're still okay. Sorry. I tried to add some Tabasco to cover the taste a bit. How many chicken legs do you want?" I sign to Davis that she burned the beans and he responds to her, "Ms. Sales, I'm sure it's fine. I've never had one bad meal here."

"I'm not really that hungry, Mama," I whisper, and then sit down on my orange chair. Davis sits down beside me as I translate for him. He signs back, "Three. You're not hungry?"

"Davis wants three. Like I said, I'm not really hungry."

"Is it because I burned the beans?" She asks me, turning around then sitting down at the table, two plates of food firmly in her hands.

"No, my stomach isn't feeling good, that's all. I didn't sleep last night and that usually messes up my stomach." Putting the plates down, then pushing one towards Davis and one towards me, she says, "Well, the Tabasco sauce is good for that." Instead of replying, my eyes avert to that place in the kitchen again. I gently touch the scar on my head again ... then think of why Erick's neck is marked with a jagged scar.

"Thanks for cooking dinner. I'll try some beans," I say with a sincere smile, followed by a fatigued sigh.

"Wow, I so needed that! Can you please tell my mom how to cook like this? She only cooks chicken breasts, always takes the skin off the chicken, and then bakes it until it's dryer than a desert. It doesn't taste like anything," Davis exclaims, fifteen minutes later. Mama signs back, "Thank you." One of the few words she knows in Sign.

After dinner, we view the pictures from my trip. I don't remember having taken so many, but there are two-hundred and twenty pictures. Esperanza ended up doing most of the photo shooting. I'm not really smiling in many of them. Of course Davis and Mama both keep on asking me why I can never smile. Pictures click and go. As we slowly enjoy the slideshow, I start thinking about last night. About my birthday party. About the past semester at Stonehill ...and about fears ...

A picture of Erick talking, while my arms are crossed and I am rolling my eyes ... One of Esperanza and I in front of Casablanca ...

... Much of my anger has come from my own ignorance of myself. Of how I arrived here; not just geographically, but how I came to be me. Do I even know who "me" really is? I thought I did, up until Erick had flung those little yellow pills at me. But how is it possible to blossom, fully into me, when there are parts of me that are not allowed to be known? To be realized?

A picture of me and Chinua, sticking our tongues out at the camera.

... What would it mean to be me? To fully be me, formed by my awareness of everything? My fear to love women? My fear of divulging to Mama and Davis, my new memories of my fourth birthday? Of a man who is supposed to be that other half of me? ...A picture of my back to the camera, as I talk to mama on Erick's cell phone ...

What happens when I am no longer fearful of a symphony, sometimes a cacophony, of *truthsongs*? What, then, does Savannah Penelope Sales become?

... a picture of Erick, holding up the Annie brass keychain he had purchased for a ridiculous twelve dollars. He is holding it just below his neck, near the scar he had gotten from being attacked and raped in Boston, nearly seven years ago ...

I reach into the pocket of my hoodie, feeling a half of a broken yellow pill I had decided to keep, "...I still feel the pain, every fifteenth of the month. I'm twenty-one again. It's 2000, August 15th, 2:15 am. I remember the putrid smell of the alley, the knife, the pain, blood ... him tearing into me, trying to be inside of me ..."

... A picture of Esperanza and I on the Metro, doing a peace sign with our fingers ...

How does Savannah Penelope Sales re-member herself, through truth songs of the past, present, and future? Can I be whole again? Even with scars?

… The last picture is a close up of my face and scar, taken by Erick, in front of Port Authority, earlier today …

Every time they would look at my forehead, and see that scar, it constantly reopened the wounds of a day everyone had remembered except me. All this time, I had mistaken their looks as being rooted in pity. However, it had been love and protection … and they suffered too.

"Looks like you had a good time, despite the lack of smiles," Davis says. Looking at his watch, he yawns, "I should get back home. There's an ice warning for after ten, so I shouldn't be out too late." He closes his laptop and then stands up. We give him a hug goodnight and tell him to drive safely.

"God I love that kid. Can't wait until he becomes my son-in-law," Mama says jokingly.

Though I'm about to pass out from fatigue, and my body wants to go to bed, my heart decides differently. I open my mouth, breath slowly and deeply into my belly … then exhale and reach out for Mama's hand.

It's time to re-member.

PART II: RE-MEMBERING

CHAPTER SEVENTEEN

I tell her about my birthday memories and the reoccurring nightmare I have had for the past three years. She hugs me and cries. She asks me why I could not tell her about the dreams. I tell her that I wanted to protect her from ever having to feel regrets for doing what she had to do for us. I tell her that she no longer has to keep it a secret on how she was able to pay Scott for this apartment.

"Baby, had I known about your nightmares, I would have told you sooner. I didn't know, baby. Please forgive me. I didn't know that that's what you've been dreaming about." She cries some more, and hugs me tighter, struggling to breathe through her tears. I massage her chest with my hand, whispering to her that I love her, worried that the crying will obstruct her breathing.

"I'll bring you your oxygen and some catnip tea, Mama," I eventually say.

"Thank you honey," she replies, squeezing my hand as I stand up.

"I love you," she mouths. I smile and head to the kitchen.

***

"Sometimes not remembering is important to heal, depending on where you are in life's journey, Savi. And sometimes it's not. In this case, I honestly thought it was necessary that you not have my memories of Scott. Up until your fourth birthday, I thought I had been able to protect you from him. I wanted you to develop in a way that was not hindered by the truth of who your father was, what he had done to me, and my life in Georgia. I didn't want you to think that the Sales's legacy was all about failure and pain … and that that was all you had to look forward to. I was eventually going to tell you when you were a little older, but now I regret that I didn't tell you sooner. I just didn't want you to be ashamed. Children are so impressionable."

She says she had feared that if I knew I had a white father, I would figure out or remember that Scott *is* my father. So, when I was about six years old and had wondered why I was much lighter than

Mama, this is what she had told me, "Your father was a very light skinned brotha. Case closed. Our people come in all different hues."

She also had feared that being born and raised in a household that was "always a paycheck away from poverty," with an abusive and alcoholic father, and a mother who would "cower at everything he did and said," would not be "good for my soul."

She tells me that about four months before she would find herself in Connecticut, her mother and twin sister would die at the hands of her father's alcoholism in 1987. An evening after he had been drinking at the local bar, he had gone to pick up her mother and sister, Daisy, from the diner at which they had been waiting tables. Later that Saturday evening, she had received a phone call from her father's sister, crying that my drunken grandfather had driven his truck through a red light and that they had been hit by a cement truck. Daisy and my grandmother were killed instantly, while my grandfather, Clarence, survived with an amputated right leg, paraplegia, and permanent brain damage.

"My aunt Iris, my father's sister, had to sell our house in order to pay for daddy to be cared for, which meant I had no place to live except with aunt Iris ... and she was just as loathsome and as screwed up as daddy." Because the car accident had left Mama's father severely brain damaged, her aunt legally became in charge of his financial affairs. Angry that her aunt sold the house to pay for medical care she felt her father did not deserve, Mama dropped out of high school less than two weeks away from graduating and two months before her eighteenth birthday. A day after dropping out of school, and four months after the death of her mother and sister, she decided to leave her aunt's house. A little less than nine months before I would be born, she departed from the local bus station in Buena Vista, Georgia.

"I was young, hated myself, hated my family, hated I had dropped out of school, hated that I had nothing. I left my town, pissed and resentful, with four hundred dollars I had stolen from my aunt Iris, a small suitcase, a photo album of pictures of just Daisy and me, and a framed picture of Daisy and me from our sixteenth birthday. I wanted to forget everything but her. She was all I had and my father's alcoholism and mother's cowardly approach to his 'one-screw-up-after-another' way of life, took her away from me. When I left Georgia, I wanted to forget everything about Buena Vista except Daisy. She wasn't supposed to die. I was the screw-up. I had pathetic grades in school. I hated school but she worked hard at school and got good grades, all while waiting tables at the diner ever since she had turned fifteen. She was supposed to go to Georgia State University. Had even gotten early acceptance and a good nursing school scholarship. First in our family who would have gone to college. Daddy would have been picking up all three of us from the diner, had I not quit one week earlier.

"When I got to the bus station, I told the clerk, 'Put me on the next bus. I don't care where it goes.'"

That 'next bus' would depart for Hartford, Connecticut.

"I met Scott Forsythe at the Blue Shirt, a restaurant and pub with live jazz music. It was across the street from the bus and train station in Hartford. After a twenty-hour trip, I decided to get some dinner there. He was in a trio, playing the drums, but I didn't notice him because I was at my booth alone; looking miserable and sad throughout my dinner, staring at my picture of Daisy and I." She says she was too young and inexperienced to differentiate 'between a shepherd and a wolf.'

"After his gig was over, Scott, thirty-six at the time, sat down at my table and said, 'Hey sweetheart, I noticed you're looking a little sad. What gives?' I thought he really cared, but would later learn it was the same tactic he used on many 'desperate-looking' young girls he wanted to sleep with.

"He was very charming and quite gorgeous. Shoulder length raven black hair and warm light brown bright eyes. I rarely dug white guys, but he certainly got my attention. I talked to him for hours. He paid for my meal, bought me dessert, and then offered to drive me to wherever I needed to go. I asked for him to drop me off at the closest motel since I didn't have any family or friends to stay with.

"He asked me if I had a credit card because I would need one for a motel; that it didn't matter if I had cash on me. I began to cry because I didn't. He offered that he would let the motel use his credit card and that I could give him the money later."

He helped carry her suitcase to her room and they talked some more.

"He was so easy to talk to. I was charmed by the fact that he seemed to care about me and wanted to make sure that I was okay. I was so touched by what I thought was kindness, that I burst into tears and gave him a hug. It just felt so good to hug someone I thought cared about me."

That was when Scott had made his move.

"He started caressing my back, then kissing my neck. I didn't think it was weird because I just felt so comfortable with him from the 'get go.' One thing led to another … After that, we would see each other at my motel room, almost every day, for about two months.

"I wanted to finally believe my miserable life had found some happiness. I wanted to believe that I could finally forget Buena Vista. I admit it: I was in denial about him paying for my motel while we would sleep together. I convinced myself that he cared about me and that this was not 'something else.' … But then, I started noticing things that reminded me of daddy, after the first two weeks." She explains that when he would come to her, she knew he was drunk, but "held himself rather well." She said that she eventually asked him to not drink "so much" before seeing her. It reminded her of how her mother and sister had died.

"Instead of sympathizing, he yelled at me. He told me to mind my own business and that he was a grown man who knew how to handle his liquor. I screamed at him and called him an asshole. He smacked me in the face, and then he left." I shudder, and hug my mama tighter.

"It's hard for me too … I understand if it's too much to hear everything right now, Savi. Want me to stop?"

Sniffling, I reply, "I'm okay."

"Daddy used to get that way with my mother, every time she would 'kindly' ask him not to drink so much."

But, she says she didn't know what to do. He was paying for her motel and she had run out of money and wouldn't start her new waitressing job for a few days. However, he returned to her room the next morning, sober, with roses, apologies, and what she thought was a smile of sincerity.

"He begged for my forgiveness and told me how he couldn't lose me; that he was madly in love with me. I believed him ... just like my mother used to believe my father after hitting her for the umpteenth time. I needed to believe that he couldn't possibly be the same as daddy."

After that, things were okay for about six more weeks. Then, one evening, she knew he had been with someone else, before coming to see her. He smelled like beer and he had "faint remainders" of lipstick on the back of his neck.

"I asked him about it. He told me that he wasn't 'that drunk;' that a 'groupie' from the audience had kissed him on the neck while he was sitting down at the bar with his band. But I knew he had slept with her, and then once again had driven to my motel room, drunk.

"I was upset and yelled at him that he would end up dead or crippled if he didn't stop drinking and driving. I told him that I loved him—well, I thought that what we had was 'love' at the time—and didn't want him ending up the same way my family had. I told him I knew he was lying about the kiss on his neck. I called him a 'whore ...'" She stops and is quiet for about thirty-seconds.

"It's okay Mama," I whisper. Her slender ebony brown fingers grace her cheekbone as she remembers what happened next.

"He hit me. Punched me in the face, then left. I had run away a thousand miles, back into the exact same situation my mother had been in. It wasn't until that very evening that I stopped hating my mother. Finally, I realized how scary it was to both stay and leave—especially if you had two little ones and were financially dependent on your guy. Yes, I was my mother on both accounts; earlier that morning, I had learned that I was pregnant with you.

"I stayed up all night, crying. I had packed my bags and tried to convince myself to leave. However, with my Baptist upbringing, I was convinced that God was punishing me, for laying down with a man before marriage, and for leaving my crippled father behind.

"He arrived the next morning with flowers. He apologized and I told him I was pregnant. He promised to never hit me again, said he'd pay for an abortion, said I should move into his place—

which I had never been to by the way—and then asked me to marry him.

"When he proposed, I realized that God was testing me, but not for what I had cried over, the previous night. Love has its trials and tribulations. God was testing me to choose love in a way I had never thought of before. That morning, I chose to love, honor, and cherish." She pauses and asks me again if I'm doing "okay." I tell that her I'm fine and say that it's okay for her to continue.

"I didn't choose Scott." Instead, her choice for the recipient of her love would be herself and me.

"Why would he want me to get an abortion, yet still marry him? I knew he was lying. He didn't want marriage. He didn't want our baby. God knows how many girls he had in motels, waiting around for him, and thinking he loved us.

"So, I lied to him. I told him I'd marry him then asked if he could get me something for my bruised cheek, down at the drugstore." As soon as he left, she tore out the Yellow Pages' listings of local shelters, grabbed her luggage, and "prayed to God" that she would have somewhere to sleep that night.

"I don't care what women choose to do when they are pregnant. I can't make that choice for them because I'm not them. But me? I chose to keep you. It never crossed my mind not to keep you. I want you to know that you were never a mistake, Savi. Scott was the mistake. I've loved you ever since I knew you were inside of me. You were not an 'unexpected pregnancy'; you were an 'unexpected blessing' and I never had any regrets."

That following spring, I was born. During her pregnancy and time spent at a halfway house for pregnant teens, she had learned that Scott had been searching for her at various shelters. She also learned, from one of the counselors at the house, that Scott had a criminal record. However, she tells me that she doesn't need me to know anymore about that.

"Please tell me everything. I need to know, Mama." She mentally deliberates on my request for a half of a minute. As I wait, I feel the desire to vomit. The beans I had for dinner begin to twist and jump in my stomach. I reach over to get my cup of catnip tea from off of the coffee table. After a few sips, I am able to regain my constitution for the moment. Mama nods to herself that it is time to continue.

"He had gone to jail for a year for the statutory rape of three teens when he was in his early twenties and living in Wisconsin. Got a short one-year sentence because his father was wealthy and could afford excellent lawyers to convince the jury that Scott had not known that the girls were 'girls.' How the hell does a twelve year old and two thirteen year old girls not look like little girls to a grown ass man?" she asks in disgust, shaking her head.

"A year after getting out of jail, he moved to Los Angeles, stalked a teenage girl who was working at a restaurant there, and then landed back in jail because of it." She pauses, asks me if I'm okay again, and then continues.

Upon realizing that she had become pregnant by Scott, while under the age of eighteen, her case worker demanded that Mama have him arrested for statutory rape, a week after I was born.

"I'm not going to lie. I still had love for him. Even after I learned of all the miserable things he had done, I did have love for him. I didn't want him to go to jail. I told her that everything we did was consensual; that he had not forced me to do anything I did not want to do. However, I started getting worried when she told me that if he had been searching for me, there was no telling what he would do if he found out I had had my baby and he would have to pay child support. I told her I didn't want anything from him. My caseworker just laughed at me, then said something like, 'What the hell are you going to do without a high school diploma, no job, and no money? You need to contact his father then. They're incredibly loaded.' Then, she threatened to have the state take you away if I didn't tell the police that Scott was your father because she said I was putting you in danger. So, I told the police, but only to protect you from him, that's all. I didn't do it because I wanted anything from Scott or his rich father." Her caseworker was not satisfied. She had expected Mama to seek out the possibility of child support from Scott's father, but Mama refused.

"Damn I annoyed Bertie—that was my caseworker's name. I think she had it in her head that I wasn't ashamed about what I had done. Why should I be? Mind you, this was nearly twenty years ago, this white woman with a Master's in social work from Smith College, thought it okay to tell me that I was yet 'another irresponsible Black teen mother with no values.' I don't think you can get away with saying that racist crap in 2007—or maybe you can? Anyway, it was the 1980s and the Reagan administration made sure that anyone who wasn't perfect white Pollyanna was seen as 'the problem' in the eyes of the status quo. She told me she would make sure that the state gained custody of you until I got my act together. And then she said I should feel ashamed for even having "enticed" a man nearly old enough to be my father.

"Bertie told me she was sick of people like me. Not people like Scott, but people like me. Immoral Black girls were 'the problem,' not the Scotts of the world. I remember finally losing my calm and calling her 'cunt.' She told me to apologize to her. Hell no I didn't. Then, she gave me 'til the end of the day to apologize. If I still hadn't groveled for her forgiveness by then, she said she would put you into a foster home and I would be kicked out." Living in New Haven at the time, she decided to leave.

"I guess I was hot headed and stupid and just couldn't apologize. I thought she didn't deserve it. So, I left her office, packed up the suitcase, and then left the house. At that time, I would rather be homeless on the streets then have them take you away from me. I vowed to love, honor, and cherish you. I felt that I could protect you on my own, without Bertie's help."

For about nine months, she bounced from shelter to shelter. At the beginning, it was easier for her to find a shelter than it was for homeless women without newborn babies. However, every time someone at the shelter would suggest she put me up for adoption or into foster care, she would become paranoid that they'd take me away in middle of the night. So, her impulse was to leave immediately, and she did. Unfortunately, there were just so many shelters that she could go to, especially during the winter when there were many more people seeking shelter; they feared they would freeze to death at night, out on the streets.

When she had left Scott, she tells me, she never fathomed that she would ever have to use her body for 'special arrangements' again. She had promised God that she would never let anything happen to me; that she would never be in the same situation that she had been with Scott. However, we had been living on the street for three days, unable to find a shelter, and she said she knew plenty of girls who were selling themselves for a warm night in a stranger's bed.

"It was the worse time to be without shelter and food, as Connecticut was being hit with what seemed like never ending torrential rain and ice storms. I thought we could endure it ... but then on that third night, the temperature dropped down to the coldest night of the year. I knew if we stayed outside that night, we would not make it ... and you were sick." She hugs me tighter, shivering as her body remembers that cold bitter night.

"The next morning, we woke up here, in this apartment." I breathe slowly and deeply, preparing myself for the story of how she would have to sell her body to gain shelter and safety for us. I don't know what I would have done. It just doesn't seem right. Why didn't anyone just help her out of kindness? Why do men think all we have to offer is sex?

Mama tells me that a few months earlier, she had ended up talking to a man she had met at Friendly's restaurant. It was another time she had been in between shelters. She had brought us there so she could use the five dollars she had gotten, while begging, for something to eat. The manager of the restaurant did not want to give her a booth because she looked "unclean and unkempt." A man sitting at a booth overheard the conversation.

"He got up from his booth and told the manager that I was welcomed to sit at his booth. So, we did. We sat there for about an hour. You slept beside me. I didn't talk too much because I thought he was probably just like Scott. He was in his late forties and didn't talk too much throughout the hour. He said his parents owned real estate throughout Connecticut that he managed it. Mostly apartments and small office buildings. He paid for my lunch and told me that maybe he could work something out if I needed a cheap place to live, with no down payment. He asked me if I'd like to hear 'the proposal' and I immediately told him, 'Thanks but no thanks,' because I assumed he'd want the same thing that Scott had wanted. He didn't push me for a reason, just gave me his business card anyway. I laughed as I saw that his name was Scott Wrentham Paulson. He had introduced himself as 'Wren,' but I guess that that was his nickname. I thanked him for the meal. He asked if he could drive us somewhere. I told him that I didn't take rides from strangers, thanked him again for the meal, and then left.

"Three months later, while at the bus stop in Waterbury, in that storm, I reached into my coat pocket to find a used tissue for my running nose. You were ten months old, in between my coat and bosom, and you wouldn't stop crying and coughing. I knew you were freezing and coming down with a cold. I pulled out that card I had forgotten about and had thought I'd thrown away. I asked God to forgive me, then went to the pay phone beside the bus stop to use my last quarter. I had to lie to myself and think, 'Maybe he wouldn't be like Scott. Maybe he really wants to help us with no strings attached.' But I just couldn't believe it in my heart. Other than my body, what did I have to offer a forty-something year old man with an MBA in real estate management? He had repeatedly told me how pretty and beautiful I was, while we ate at Friendly's. Who was he fooling?" *Oh God, maybe I don't need to hear anymore of this story.* Mama becomes acutely aware that I have potentially reached my threshold to hear any more. She whispers, "Have some more tea," and then nudges me to pour more catnip from the *Bodum* glass teapot that Davis's mama gave her last Christmas. Ten seconds later, I am slowly sipping the soothing liquid. After about a minute, I begin to feel more relaxed and less anxious.

"Okay, I'm cool now. It's cool," I tell Mama.

"Scott Wrentham Paulson was living in Hebron at the time. He came and got us. He told me he would drive us to this place called East Lebanon, Connecticut, next to Hebron. As soon as he picked us up, he wanted to talk about his proposal, just to make sure I was okay with it. But, I told him that I didn't want to hear it until we got to the apartment.

"We drove to the middle of nowhere. I started panicking and thinking, 'What if he's a serial killer? How stupid was I to believe he's taking us to a place to live?' I kept on wondering if I had any type of weapon on me. I wasn't thinking right. I was sleep deprived, food deprived, everything deprived. I realized that I had called him out of desperation and deprivation. Until that point, I had not fathomed that he could actually kill us. But, my fears partially subsided when he pulled into the small parking lot of an apartment building.

"He led us up to a unit—this unit—while carrying a black duffel bag. When we got here, the apartment was furnished. He gave me the duffel bag and told me, 'Maybe you'll feel better if you take a hot bath and eat. Then, we can talk about how this can be your new home.' I went into the bathroom and gave you a bath in the sink. The bag had some soap in it, some diapers, wipes, baby food, formula, sandwiches, and even cold medicine for babies. I thought it was kind of strange that he bought stuff for you. Wasn't he only interested in me? But then I quickly told myself, "Of course he's interested in treating both of us well if he wants what I think he wants ..." I took a shower, then I put on the sweatshirt and sweatpants he had put in the duffel bag.

"'Now you look like a beautiful clean young lady,' he told me, as I came out of the bathroom with you asleep in my arms. Then he said something like, 'Sorry I didn't have any baby clothes for her. They just had food and medicine at the 7-Eleven, this late at night. We used to give my daughter that stuff when she had a cold as a baby. It seemed to help. If that cough of hers doesn't get any better, let me know if you want me to take you two to Windham Hospital, okay?' I started becoming confused. Like I said, I was severely tired, hungry, etc., and probably delirious and hallucinating.

"'So, do you want to go to bed now?' he asked me. That's when I lost it. I started crying uncontrollably and told him I didn't want to sleep with him and begged him to take me back to the bus station. I told him I couldn't let God down; that I thought I could do it but I couldn't sell myself to him.

"His eyes became wide with surprise and his mouth gaped open. I thought to myself, 'Shit, he's pissed and he's going to hurt us.' He stood up from the sofa, rather abruptly, a look of confusion on his face. He told me he wasn't going to hurt me. I remember screaming as he took a step towards us, then I passed out."

I brace myself for the story of how she let God down. The ending is obvious, simply from the reoccurring dreams I have had for the past several years; obvious because that is how these types of stories always end. *These men don't care about us, only what's in between our legs*, I think angrily. But, I had to know. I had to hear from her what she was forced to do, simply because this rich white man, who could have given her this apartment for free, wanted to more.

CHAPTER EIGHTEEN

January 18, 1989

My eyes open. I blink several times, trying to understand where my body is. I am lying on my back in a very bright room. Turning my head, I see my angel sleeping beside me, sucking on her left thumb—

—Wren! What happened to Wren? Oh my God, did he do it!?

I sit straight up in the bed, throw the covers off of me, and realize that I am fully clothed. *Why did he put clothes back on me after he did it? I wonder with panic.*

Why do I feel okay? It doesn't feel like he did anything 'down there'—

Coughing. I hear coughing beyond the door. *It must be Wren,* I think. My nineteen-year-old heart is beating so fast, I think it is going to burst through my chest.

There is a note taped to the bedroom door. Quietly, I leave the bed and tip toe to the door.

> *Lily,*
>
> *I did not mean to scare you. I know it is only my word, but I would never and could never hurt you or your baby. I can only imagine what has happened in your life that that is what you saw in me. It pains my heart that someone can hurt God's children. You're just a child and shouldn't have to be scared of anything.*
>
> *—Wren*

My eyes read the note five times, but I refuse to believe it. Shaking my head, I whisper, "How can this be?" I turn around and then look at Savannah, the love of my life. I walk over to her and gently lay my hand on her forehead, checking for a fever. However, she feels cool. Her eyes—those big beautiful light brown eyes—open and look up at me.

"Good morning poopie bear," I whisper. Like she always does when she wakes up, her arms reach out to be picked up, given a kiss, and then hugged. Two-seconds later, she is firmly in my arms, pressed up against my bosom. I tell her that I am sorry if I scared her when I screamed. I ask her to forgive me for almost having broken my promise to both her and to God. I tell her that Wren says he won't hurt us.

And I tell her that I love her.

***

Savannah is in my arms as we make our way out of the bedroom. I see Wren is sitting at the sofa, hands folded, looking down at something on the coffee table. Savi coughs. Wren slowly raises his head; his somber and tired eyes meet mine.

"Are you two okay?" he asks us. I nod, then remain standing in front of the bedroom door, not sure what to do.

"It's okay. Take your time. I understand," he whispers, then looks back down at whatever had been occupying his attention, before I had come into the living room.

I kiss Savannah on the forehead then take one small step towards the sofa. With that one small step, a floodgate of memories starts to replay in my head.

… My fifth birthday party with Daisy at grandma Rose's house. Daddy is there, yelling at my grandma that he does not want to give her back the money she lent him for the mortgage, but really used it for gambling … and lost.

I take another step.

I am eight years old, and daddy slaps mama in the face then calls her a list of disgusting names because she let Daisy and I share the last piece of fried chicken when he wanted it. "They didn't pay for the damn chicken so why do you think they should have it?"

Another step.

Daisy is screaming as daddy beats me with an electrical cord because I have emptied all his alcohol into the toilet. We are ten years old.

A closer step.

Mama, Daisy, and I are in the living room, celebrating Daisy's first period, over homemade oatmeal cookies, while listening to a Jackson Five album. It is 1982. Daddy comes into the living room and asks us what 'all this noise is about?' I tell him and ask if he wants to join us. He tells Daisy she is "a woman now" then asks her if she'll be "a whore like your mother was."

Another step.

My mother slaps me. She tells me I am lying. I tell her I am not. She slaps me again and tells me that my father would never do 'that.' But I do not stop telling her the truth, because I am not lying and she knows it. She slaps me again as I tell her how he has made Daisy and I touch him for years, when she works second shift. I have just turned fifteen.

My mind wrestles with my past and the pain that mama could never protect Daisy and I from; the never-ending pain that daddy gave all of us. The pain that I never want Savannah to experience or know about.

Wren looks up at us again, gives me a smile, nods, and then looks back down at what appears to be a picture. I stand in the middle of the living room for about fifteen or twenty more minutes, as my memories try not to bleed into the present. I try to tell myself, 'Wren is not Daddy. Wren is not Scott Forsythe. Wren is not Daddy. Wren is not Scott Forsythe.'

Finally, I glide across the living room, my legs winning over my memories. I give Savi a kiss on the forehead as she tries to wiggle out of my arms. I put her down onto the floor. My angel giggles, and then begins exploring the living room carpet with her tiny fingers. I sit down beside Wren and try to relax.

"Is she your daughter?" I ask him, as I look at his picture of a girl a few years younger than myself.

"Greta. She never liked the name, so we called her 'Louie.' Her middle name was 'Louise' and she thought 'Louie' was cuter than 'Louise.'" I understand immediately and whisper, "How did you lose her?"

I listen as he tells me how she never came home from her friend Anne's house, after she had dinner there. He whispers how it was the worse three months of he and his wife's lives, as they prayed that she would walk through their door at any minute. On October 21, 1985, and ninety-seven days after she had been reported missing, her body had been found in White River Junction, Vermont. Two weeks later, the FBI arrested Laurence Parks, fifty-three years old, who had already served time for being charged with child molestation, thirty years earlier. Parks had been living in a state mental institute for twelve years, after being released on probation. He was placed in a state-run psychiatric institution, to facilitate further rehabilitation and to protect society from him while he "recovered" from his "mental disease." That is, until the Reagan administration made major budget cuts that forced many state funded mental institutions to shut down, leaving their residents with no place to go to continue rehabilitation. Parks was one of these people.

A month after Greta's funeral, his wife would have a nervous breakdown. She has been in a catatonic state, at a private mental hospital in Mansfield, ever since then. He visits her nearly every day.

"When I saw you at Friendly's, I knew you were alone and I knew that you should not be. Despite being eighteen, you looked about thirteen or fourteen years old. So young ..." He takes a moment to collect his thoughts, then continues, "I didn't want to risk that someone hurt you or your baby, simply because I didn't help when I knew I should have and could have. I didn't want to seem pushy, just wanted to see how I could help. I just wanted to let you know that I could help you. I'm sorry that I initially wasn't more straightforward. It was awkward for me at the time, too." The day our paths crossed had been the anniversary of when his daughter had been found. He was on his way to her gravesite when he decided to stop at Friendly's, Greta's favorite restaurant.

"Sorry too. You offered several times to tell me about how Savi and I could have an apartment, but I kept on saying 'no' because I just assumed that you'd want ... well, you know. Same with last night when I wanted to wait until we got here."

We are quiet for several minutes. We watch Savannah crawl around, try to stand up and walk, fall down, crawl, then attempt to stand up and walk again.

"She's beautiful," he tells me, as Savi decides to walk-fall-walk-fall towards us, then gestures for me to pick her up. I scoop her up as he begins to explain how this place can become our new home. He tells me about Mrs. Lorraine Chapman, who has always enjoyed babysitting the tenants' children for free. He tells me about how he can get me a job as a janitor and cook in the kitchen of East Lebanon high school, as long as I promise him that I will attend night school to obtain my GED. He tells me that I have one year to work hard and to save up my money. He tells me of a sweet family named the Allens, who he buys his milk from. He has known the father, Davison Paul Allen II (who goes by 'Paul'), since high school. The Allens are looking for extra helping hands for their weekend work. They have four children, but their youngest is about Savannah's age, named Davis.

"I told them about you on the phone this morning, explained the situation, and they said they would love to meet you when you're ready."

Lastly, he tells me that, other than Ginger and Paul Allen, no one else can know about this arrangement, including his elderly parents who own the property.

"I love my parents dearly, but they're from a different generation and they have their opinions about Blacks and 'handouts'—which this is not, but they wouldn't understand. Don't worry, they rarely, if ever, come around here. I collect the rent from the tenants and I make sure things get fixed around here. After a year is over, I will give you a new lease to sign in which the rent will be half of what it should be. You mustn't tell anyone—not even Savannah. She may accidentally tell a neighbor and then I'll have a problem on my hands."

He smiles as Savannah grabs one of his fingers and giggles.

"May she always be happy and safe," he whispers.

I do not know it now, but in less than two years, he will pass away from a heart attack at the age of fifty-one, while visiting the grave of his only child.

CHAPTER NINETEEN

Davis is awake, lying on his side and looking at me, smiling.

I am glad he stayed the night. I am glad that he is in my life. I am glad that, for the first time in years, we can fall asleep beside each other and I trust that he doesn't "want more."

"How long have you been awake?" I ask.

"Fifteen, maybe twenty-minutes. Was watching you sleep."

"That's boring," I say, followed by a yawn.

"You looked at peace. I haven't seen that in a long time."

"I slept good. Before I fell asleep, I was worried Mama was going to find out you didn't sleep in the living room like you're supposed to, whenever you stay over."

"That's before she knew you weren't into guys. Do you think she really meant for me to crash out on the sofa, even after you told her you like girls the other night? Have you thought about what she asked you?"

"Is it because of what you saw? Do you think that did it?" I had not expected her to ask me if my love for women was connected to the trauma of my fourth birthday. I had thought about it, but it did not make any sense.

"I'm going to tell her that I don't think my love for women needs explanation. It's not a symptom of something bad that is in me or happened to me. Love—true unconditional love—is simply a symptom of love." Up until this week, I had not thought that way about myself. Erick helped me understand this when we were in Troy's bathroom, four days ago.

"Not only did my father suggest it was my fault for being raped, he suggested that there was something wrong with me for wanting to love men, and that my attacker must have seen something in me that made me deserving of it. Savi, don't ever let anyone make you think that your capacity to share your love with women is a symptom of something wrong with you. How can love ever be wrong? How could your love for someone as beautifully spirited as Esperanza, be a symptom of anything else but love?" It was one of the most powerful things he had ever said to me, because he truly believed it. Regardless of the fact that his parents had disowned him after having come out, a year before his attack, he never lost sight that the capacity to love is a priceless gift.

"Was just wondering about how you felt about what she asked you … But I like your response. Was just curious …" We are silent for about minute, and then he touches my scar with his fingertip.

Though he hadn't seen everything, he had seen enough that day. On March 24th, 1992, Mr. and Mrs. Allen were walking up the stairs to our apartment. Mr. Allen was holding Davis in his arms to make sure Davis didn't slip on the partially ice-covered stairs. After ringing the doorbell and waiting for about thirty-seconds, Mr. Allen opened the front door that Scott had left unlocked. Davis still in Mr. Allen's arms, they entered the kitchen to look for us.

"I remember seeing you on the floor and that there was blood all over your face and your eyes were closed. You mother was on her back, eyes closed too, blood coming out of her nose and her dress was up. I only saw it for about two-seconds before Dad turned around, handed me to mom, and then she took me to your bedroom. She told me not to come out until she got me, then closed the door," Davis had said last night, after I told him the re-membering that Mama and I did together, the night before last. He had told me that he didn't think he was too traumatized; just confused why his parents told him that it was important that he never tell me what he had seen; only that I had fallen and hit my head while we were playing. He also told me, "I honestly never knew that the guy who did that to your mom was your dad." His parents kept it a secret from him as well. We're silent again. Several minutes go by.

"Do you think that is why you hate us so much? From what you saw him do? It's as if every one of us is Scott Forsythe; as if we have nothing to offer you but a burden. I'm not saying racism doesn't exist, as you'd have to be a moron to not see it with Hurricane Katrina, or with the ass-wipes who hung the nooses on that tree in Jena last year. You know I was the first person to say those guys would get away with it because they're white and it's Louisiana. And you know how much it drives me crazy when those rich white Hollywood girls, like Paris, get away with everything."

"I know. It's just so hard for me to trust. It hurts so much, you know?"

"I know, but I worry about how you can enjoy life if that's all you see. I'm not saying there aren't people like Scott or the creep from Quikstop out there—which you should have told me about sooner by the way—but that's not everyone. There's also Wren, me, my father, my brothers, and Professor Rogards."

"Logically, I know this, but I just haven't been able to feel it for most of my life."

"How can I help you see this, Savi? How can I help you not just see, but believe that we all don't want to hurt you? That some of us are sick of the scars too?"

I sigh, thinking about how Mama had finally shared her life story and told me of the two Scotts that had profoundly changed our lives. One for the worse ... and one for the better.

"I'm beginning to understand this now," I sign back, the memory of Erick's tears from our night on the bathroom floor, less than a week ago, entering my consciousness. I had told Davis about Erick's scars too. And even though I do hold strong to my belief that Erick is not completely exonerated from the fact that he has a privileged perception of life that has made communication between us often hurtful and difficult ...

... I also shouldn't ignore that he has a soul that both suffers and loves ...

... and reached out to me because he knew my soul—and his—needs to heal as well.

"How can I help you feel it? How can I help you believe?" Davis whispers.

***

Later that morning, I call Esperanza. I tell her everything that has happened, since that morning she found Erick and I asleep on the bathroom floor, but had not said a word.

"I'm sorry," I tell Esperanza.

"For what?"

"For never truly seeing your scars and helping you heal."

"I don't understand."

"Sometimes we get so trapped in our own pain, we handle it in two extremes: we either ignore it, and believe that if we never talk about it, those scars will disappear. Or, we only focus on the pain that others have caused us while we simultaneously forget that others suffer too. Sometimes, we don't realize we are causing them to suffer. The key is to not forget our own pain and the pain of others, all while we all try to heal together. All while we understand that one person's pain may be rooted in another's pleasure … and one's pleasure may be built on another person's pain. The key is to try to heal together, while never losing sight of the bigger picture. I'm working on it. I know I need to do this, but I'm working on feeling and believing that this is possible." My fists clench tightly as I resist hanging up on her. *I must not hang up. I have to…I have to stop running away.* I take a really deep breath, close my eyes, and then pause for several seconds before continuing.

"Every time Mama sees the scar on my forehead it's like when you see an ad for Coca-Cola or *Hershey's* chocolate; they're crappy reminders of what happens when someone we love has been hurt by exploitation or addiction. The scars created are ugly and not always immediately visible. We can't begin to find love again if we think our scars are the only ones that exist; if we only respond to our own scars, but do not reflect on the fact that we may be simultaneously creating scars for somebody else, we're part of the problem."

She doesn't say anything for a long time. Finally, I hear her sniffling.

"Are you okay?" I ask her. Through sniffles she tells me, "I'm jumping in the car right now to drive over there and give you a hug!"

EPILOGUE

April 4, 2007
9:05 am

Dear Diary,

    I'm still angry.
    And I still yell at Erick for being oblivious about his white privilege. Not nearly as much as I used to, but I still 'check him' on his behavior. But we're cool, and he is trying. It helps that I see him for more than just the assumptions I had made about him, when we first met, and he made that comment about Vail. Yeah, he's a white boy with privilege, but he's no longer one dimensional to me. He has scars too. I think what bothered him the most about me, when we first met, was that he knew he was privileged, but it wasn't enough to "protect" him from being stabbed, raped, and contracting HIV, after walking home from a gay club, 7 years ago. Some sicko had been targeting young gay males, who were leaving dance clubs alone, throughout Massachusetts and Rhode Island, for about a year. He was eventually caught, a year after Erick's assault. Until then, Erick had never thought he could ever be a victim of a serial rapist. "It's not supposed to happen to 'us,'" he admitted to me.
    Erick had confused that his privilege would automatically mean protection from the things that were only supposed to happen to people like me, and Mama ... and Esperanza's maternal grandmother. This was what he had confessed to me, that night in the bathroom. He had felt deep shame, every time he would look at me and have such thoughts. Deep down in his heart, he knew there had been much truth to my accusations. He's been trying to reconcile this ever since, but he simultaneously pisses me off too. I'm trying to be patient. It's hard, but I'm trying to find patience.
    And maybe I'm not quite ready to let him know that in some unexpected way, he helped me realize that I do have the capacity to love those who I had thought were my enemies ... and that we have to start healing together. But maybe I'll let him know when I'm ready.

211

It's been about two months since I started re-membering. Two months since I told Mama, Esperanza, and Davis that my amnesia had been lifted ... and that I am a fledging lesbian. It took two weeks to finally convince her that, "No Mama, people don't become gay because of trauma." Yes, she had been disappointed that Davis and I would never get married, but about two weeks later, she started asking me about any "nice girls" I had met at school. Two weeks ago, she and Ginger went to a used bookstore in Willimantic. I came home from school and there, on my desk beside a plate of homemade oatmeal cookies, was Afrekete: An Anthology of Black Lesbian Writing. *On a post-it note, she had written, "Let's start our bedtime reading together again."*

God, I love her so much.

The other morning, Esperanza and I talked on the phone. She asked that I stop referring to Scott as a 'wolf.' I was about to go off on her when I realized that I should just shut the hell up and let her have her say. She tried to tell me, as usual, about my 'oppression' of animals through the language I'm using. "Wolves are only 'evil' because people in the Western world say they are. Do you think the wolf thinks of himself as 'evil?'" I'm not really sure what the hell that has to do with my asshole of a father, but I decided to respect her wishes and this whole vegan and animal love thing she's so dedicated to. Later that evening, we met up at Violet's Cafe. She told me how Cesar Chavez—who I think is awesome—didn't believe in eating animals either. She said something like, "See, it's not just a white people thing. He thought the farm workers and animals were both getting, as you would say, 'The shit end of the shit stick.'" I even browsed through some animal lover books she gave me. Not that I'm going to stop eating my chicken and eggs any time soon, but some stuff in that Sexual Politics of Meat *got me thinking about some things I never thought about before. Esperanza invited me to an animal rights meeting at Uconn that night, but I respectfully declined. Yea, I don't really get it, but maybe that's how she's healing too.*

***

May 27, 2007
11:50 PM

Dear Diary

    I had this dream last night. Fell asleep listening to Nina Simone. There was water everywhere. I was floating, bobbing up in down, trying to keep my head above water. Erick, Mama, and Davis were there also, trying not to drown. It was weird though, because they were all holding onto things. I kept on yelling at them to let go so they don't drown. Mama was holding onto cartons of cigarettes with what appeared to be blurry pictures of Scott on them. Erick was holding onto a bunch of turtleneck shirts. Davis was balancing a tray of carrot cupcakes and wearing a party hat.

    Cesar passed by us, floating—not drowning—singing, "Save Me From the Water," and playing the piano.

    I remember looking at my body, trying to understand why, I too, was having difficulty trying not to drown. I looked down and saw that my arms were elongated, wrapped around myself. My hands were stretched back around to the front, underneath my bosom, literally padlocked to each other. My legs kicked beneath me.

    I was holding onto myself.

***

May 30, 2007
4:55 pm

Dear Diary,

    Other than the trippy dream from the other night, I haven't had those nightmares about Scott since March. I know now that I was confusing my fourth birthday party with what I had imagined had happened during Mama's 'special arrangement' with Scott 'Wren' Paulson. I guess that's pretty deep. Erick keeps on pushing for me to 'explore' this more. He's suggested that my hate towards white men plays into this and I didn't just conveniently substitute my

213

early memory of the 'good Scott' for the 'bad Scott.' "Why did you forget what had actually happened during your party and relocate that memory to create some 'evil white guy' that replaced your infant memory of the 'good' Scott? Maybe that's how you've been able to justify, to yourself, that all white men are capable of what he did?" That's what he emailed me. I emailed him back, 'Screw you.' Why does he do that to me?

Anyway, Erick has been trying to persuade me to go to therapy. He says it saved his life and I should look into what Stonehill offers for students. I don't know if I need it. Maybe I do. Feels like my new honesty with myself, with Mama, and everyone is the best therapy for me. I don't know if I would want to talk about this stuff with a complete stranger who only cares because they're being paid to care ... but I do think if I can find a brown or Black woman therapist, I would be up for it.

***

June 10, 2007
10:08 am

Dear Diary,

Yesterday, I asked Esperanza what she would think if I decided that I never want to visit Scott in prison, or ever write him and that I hope he dies soon and that I don't feel the least bit sad about it. She surprised me by saying she would probably feel the same way too. I burst into tears. I don't know why. Maybe it felt good to hear that it's okay, at least for right now, to hate my own father.

I'm still waiting for my memories to come back from that "missing" year in my life. Davis and Mama tell me I should take my time. Anyway, I have plenty of pictures from 1982-1983. Speaking of pictures, Mama and I went over her photo album of Aunt Daisy and her, for the gazillionth time, last night. All this time, that safe in her bedroom had held that album, the first two yearly leases that Wren had given her, a newspaper cut-out of a small blurb about my

214

father's arrest and twenty-five year prison sentence, and the first note Wren had ever written to her on January 18, 1989.

Guess what? Erick, Esperanza, Davis, and I are all reading this book called Enter the River: Healing Steps from White Privilege Toward Racial Reconciliation. *I didn't suggest it. Nope, Esperanza didn't suggest it. Erick—that's right, Captain America—suggested it after he said he did a search on Amazon.com, and was "shocked that so many people have written about 'this stuff.'' Maybe I should email him 'Screw you,' more often. I did think about what he had emailed me, though. Who knows, maybe there is some truth to what he wrote. He just pissed me off because he comes off being so damn 'authoritative' about everything, sometimes. Anyway, Erick and Davis have been asking Esperanza and I many questions during bowling night.*

Cesar, Troy, and Chinua came down for Erick's twenty-eighth birthday party last night. We all went to a Nigerian restaurant in East Hartford. Cesar gave me a gift. It's this very journal that I'm writing in, with his favorite muse, Audre Lorde, on the cover. He's working on a draft of the musical version of Kindred. *I think Cesar has become my secret muse.*

I close my new journal, and probably, for the twentieth time, contemplate over the truthsong written in silver script lettering, flowing across the picture of Audre Lorde:

We have chosen each other
and the edge of each other's battles
the war is the same
if we lose
someday women's blood will congeal
upon a dead planet
if we win
there is no telling
we seek beyond history
for a new and more possible meeting
—Audre Lorde[iii]

I exhale, put the journal away, and then continue packing my bags for Columbia University.

NOTES

[iii] Kirk, Gwyn, & Okazawa-Rey, Margo. (2007). *Women's lives: Multicultural perspectives* (4th ed., p. xxiv). New York: McGraw Hill.

ABOUT THE AUTHOR

A. Breeze Harper was born and raised in a working-class household in Lebanon, Connecticut, in the United States of America, with her twin, Tal. It is the town that inspired her to create the fictional "East Lebanon," in *Scars*. She has a Bachelors degree in feminist geography, from Dartmouth College, and earned her Masters degree in Educational Technologies, at Harvard University in 2007. Harper has a PhD from the University of California, Davis, where she studied applications of critical race feminism, critical whiteness studies, and critical food studies within cultural geography. When she is not writing about the complexities of identity, power, and privilege, she enjoys running, hiking, camping, vegan baking and cooking, and herbalism. Harper is also the author of the book *Sistah Vegan: Black Female Vegans Speak on Food, Identity, Health, and Society* (Lantern Books, 2010). You can learn more about her on her official website, at www.abreezeharper.com.

Printed in the United States
By Bookmasters